On Fire, Under Fire, or Fired

On Fire, Under Fire, or Fired

Superintendents in the Pandemic

Susan Enfield
Kristi Wilson

ROWMAN & LITTLEFIELD
Lanham • Boulder • New York • London

Rowman & Littlefield
Bloomsbury Publishing Inc, 1385 Broadway, New York, NY 10018, USA
Bloomsbury Publishing Plc, 50 Bedford Square, London, WC1B 3DP, UK
Bloomsbury Publishing Ireland, 29 Earlsfort Terrace, Dublin 2, D02 AY28, Ireland
www.rowman.com

Copyright © 2025 by Susan Enfield and Kristi Wilson

All rights reserved. No part of this publication may be: i) reproduced or transmitted in any form, electronic or mechanical, including photocopying, recording or by means of any information storage or retrieval system without prior permission in writing from the publishers; or ii) used or reproduced in any way for the training, development or operation of artificial intelligence (AI) technologies, including generative AI technologies. The rights holders expressly reserve this publication from the text and data mining exception as per Article 4(3) of the Digital Single Market Directive (EU) 2019/790.

British Library Cataloguing in Publication Information Available

Library of Congress Cataloging-in-Publication Data

Names: Enfield, Susan, 1968– author. | Wilson, Kristi, 1973– author.
Title: On fire, under fire, or fired : superintendents in the pandemic / Susan Enfield, Kristi Wilson.
Description: Lanham : Rowman & Littlefield, [2025] | Includes bibliographical references and index. | Summary: "In On Fire, Under Fire, or Fired: Superintendents in the Pandemic current and former superintendents reflect on the challenges and successes faced during and after the COVID-19 pandemic and share recommendations on how we can continue to learn from this historic moment and advance our public education system to serve all students"— Provided by publisher.
Identifiers: LCCN 2024046782 (print) | LCCN 2024046783 (ebook) | ISBN 9781475874983 (cloth ; alk. paper) | ISBN 9781475874990 (paperback ; alk. paper) | ISBN 9781475875003 (epub)
Subjects: LCSH: School superintendents—United States. | Educational leadership—United States. | School crisis management—United States. | COVID-19 Pandemic, 2020–2023—United States.
Classification: LCC LB2831.72 .E558 2025 (print) | LCC LB2831.72 (ebook) | DDC 371.2/011097309052—dc23/eng/20241223
LC record available at https://lccn.loc.gov/2024046782
LC ebook record available at https://lccn.loc.gov/2024046783

For product safety related questions contact productsafety@bloomsbury.com.

∞™ The paper used in this publication meets the minimum requirements of American National Standard for Information Sciences—Permanence of Paper for Printed Library Materials, ANSI/NISO Z39.48-1992.

We built a new school system from the ground up in a few weeks during the spring of 2020. Then we did it again, this time better, for online learning in the fall of 2020. Then we did it again for hybrid learning in the spring of 2021. We did this in the midst of a fractured political environment and through racial strife. This was the most intense time of our careers, but never for one moment did I see a colleague step away from the task, even when it would have been rational to do so. We had to operate under rules and conditions we never asked for. The state rules that governed returning to school in "hybrid"—combining remote and brick-and-mortar instruction—were, in many ways, the worst of both worlds, no matter how well districts planned. We made the best of it. Superintendents were some of the unsung heroes of the pandemic.

—Dr. Alan Spicciati, Superintendent, Auburn School District, Washington

Contents

Foreword		ix
Preface		xi
Acknowledgments		xiii
1	Navigating the Unknown	1
2	Connecting through the Power of Networking	17
3	Relief Funding and Its Complex Legacy: The Effects of COVID-19 on School Budgets	33
4	Creating a Culture of Care for Students and Staff	51
5	Innovating to Improve Education: Teaching and Learning in New Ways	69
6	Communicating and Partnering with Families and Community: Ties That Bond	85
7	Managing Politics While Prioritizing Students	107
8	Threats and Opportunities Moving Forward	123
Bibliography		133
Index		137
About the Authors		143

Foreword

As we reach the five-year anniversary of the start of the COVID-19 pandemic, central questions come to the surface with ever-greater urgency: What happened at that time and in the aftermath? What insights and takeaways can we learn from the experience going forward?

This book, *On Fire, Under Fire, or Fired: Superintendents in the Pandemic*, deserves a prominent place among the books that tackle these essential questions. It looks at the COVID-19 years from the unique perspective of America's K–12 school superintendents. Individuals in those positions suddenly found themselves at the center of one of the most consequential and high-impact effects of the pandemic: school closures and the shift to remote learning.

The book sheds light on the extraordinary work done by the nation's school superintendents at a time of great uncertainty and sorrow. Above all, this is a story of their resourcefulness and leadership.

As powerfully discussed in the following pages, it was the job of superintendents to manage the running and functioning of schools and school districts—while the entire nation's school system was in lockdown. They had responsibility for the safety and well-being of teachers, fellow administrators, staff, and the more than 50 million students in America.

This responsibility meant devising new food distribution methods when the provision of school meals went remote, too. It meant solving thorny tech problems to make sure that students had reliable computer devices and internet access at home and grappling with online learning programs, curriculum, and research-based metrics. There were imperatives of teacher recruiting and retention, training, setting up tutoring programs, and providing mental health support. There were, in some cases, needs for new cleaning protocols and upgrades to the HVAC systems of aging buildings.

Superintendents were in charge of budgets, fiscal operations, and record keeping, were also liaisons with government and public health officials, and frequently worked with school boards needing to balance politics and advocacy. They were the face of public education for understandably worried parents, families, and local communities, and, as such, used all their skills and training as communicators. They were called upon for information, reassurance, and conflict resolution, even when those were not always easy to provide.

As the executive director of American Association of School Administrators (AASA), The School Superintendents Association, and as a former superintendent, I have long observed superintendents working to strengthen school system leadership, advance achievements in our school communities, and prepare all students to be college, career, and life-ready.

Acknowledging the inevitable difficulties and stresses involved, I am proud of the way these goals held steady and were advanced, even during the unusual circumstances of COVID-19. I celebrate wholeheartedly the exceptional work we all did during the pandemic. Our mission is student-centered, and in myriad ways during COVID-19, we advocated for the rights of students and dedicated ourselves to providing the highest quality public education for all children.

I am honored to write this foreword. Within our shared profession, I have known and admired Susan Enfield and Kristi Wilson for many years, and I could not be happier that they have written this book, which consistently challenges, informs, and invites reflection. And in the process of writing, they did a wide range of interviews with fellow former and current superintendents, which captured voices, stories, and experiences that might otherwise have been lost.

This invaluable book looks both back to those "wild times" of the pandemic and onward to the future, exploring what we can learn and carry forward. The lessons are of leadership, collaboration, equity, educational innovation, and compassion, and none could be more important or timely.

David R. Schuler, Ed.D.
Executive Director, AASA, The School Superintendents Association,
Alexandria, Virginia

Preface

We began writing this book after having each served as superintendents for more than a decade. Being a superintendent has never been for the faint of heart, but leading during the COVID-19 pandemic posed challenges for which none of us were truly prepared. As we reflected on our own experiences and talked with our colleagues about theirs, we knew there was an important story here that needed to be told. During the pandemic, superintendents faced the dual challenge of protecting the health and safety of their communities while also ensuring that students kept learning. The decisions they made—from closing schools and transitioning to remote learning to addressing the social-emotional needs of students and staff—had profound and lasting effects.

First, we wanted to provide an honest account of what superintendents faced while leading their communities and providing essential services during this unprecedented crisis—services that students and their families might otherwise not have received. Superintendents demonstrated tremendous courage and humanity, and we hope that readers see them not only for what they did but also for who they are—people who had to make hard decisions and, in doing so, made mistakes, but never wavered in their commitment to students. Second, we wanted to preserve the historical context of COVID-19, documenting lessons learned and exploring how the pandemic has reshaped the superintendent's role. Equally important is the question of how communities will support their superintendents as they continue to advocate for public education.

The pandemic revealed both the vulnerabilities and strengths of our education system. It highlighted inequities that have long existed, such as the digital divide and food access, which were exacerbated when schools moved to remote learning. At the same time, it also fostered innovation and collaboration, spurring educators to rethink traditional approaches to teaching and learning and explore new strategies that could better serve all students.

This book is a tribute to the dedication and perseverance of school superintendents and all educators who faced the challenges of the pandemic with strength, resilience, and grace, and who continue to care deeply about the education of our children. It is our hope that these stories and insights will serve as a source of inspiration and support for current and future education leaders as they navigate the challenges that lie ahead.

Acknowledgments

The superintendents, current and former, whom we interviewed for this book are more than just colleagues; they are truly an inspiration to us. We will be forever grateful to each of them for entrusting us with their stories and giving us the privilege of sharing them.

We are indebted to Martha Bustin, who worked tirelessly to ensure we met our deadline successfully, and to Emma Garrett-Nelson for her assistance in the final stages of editing. Thanks also to Carrie Brandon and the team at Bloomsbury Publishing for believing in us and the importance of this book.

Finally, we want to thank our families and husbands, Tony Harasimowicz and Doug Wilson, for their support, encouragement, and patience.

Chapter 1

Navigating the Unknown

> It was far beyond academics, it was human life.
>
> —Dr. Scott Muri, former superintendent, Ector County Independent School District, Texas

People often ask, "What is a typical day in the life of a superintendent?" The most common response from superintendents is, "There is no such thing—each day is different." On any given day, superintendents can find themselves managing a schedule that could include attending a school soccer field opening with local athletes and then heading to visit classrooms before attending a meeting with community members to share information on an upcoming bond measure—all the while fielding calls from board members, staff, and colleagues. Then there are the days that are disrupted almost entirely by some kind of crisis—and superintendents are all too familiar with crises. From a school lockdown because of police activity in the area to a student who goes missing temporarily by simply getting on the wrong bus, superintendents know to be prepared for anything. Leading through crises has always required a unique set of skills and strategies, including clear communication, decisiveness, and empathy. The magnitude of the COVID-19 pandemic, however, thrust superintendents into unknown territory, challenging them as leaders to learn and adapt on a daily basis.

Like leaders in other sectors, superintendents tend to have a much higher tolerance for living with ambiguity and swimming in shades of gray when it comes to decision-making. They understand that waiting for absolute clarity before moving forward with a plan is not always an option. Given these realities, on its surface, the pandemic should have been just another fresh challenge for superintendents. After all, leading in a time of crisis is always hard,

Figure 1.1. Words of encouragement tied to trees by community members in Highline Public Schools. *Source*: Photograph courtesy of Susan Enfield.

but it is not impossible. The reality for most superintendents in the early days of the pandemic and school closures, however, was that they were facing a crisis like none before, which at times did feel impossible to manage.

In the same month that schools closed, McKinsey & Company published *Leadership in a Crisis: Responding to the Coronavirus Outbreak and Future Challenges*. They identified five behaviors to help leaders navigate the pandemic: organizing via a network of teams; displaying deliberate calm and bounded optimism; making decisions amid uncertainty; demonstrating empathy; and communicating effectively.[1] Superintendents interviewed here demonstrated all of these behaviors and also named the importance of agility, resilience, honesty, vulnerability, and visibility. They understood that communicating with staff and families was not just about disseminating essential information; it was about providing reassurance and clarity on what was happening in the moment and where we were all headed (see figure 1.1).

Amid the uncertainty and upheaval in the early days of the pandemic, superintendents had to demonstrate that they were prioritizing health and safety while ensuring that teaching and learning continued. They had to not only address the immediate, most pressing daily issues but also lay the foundation for what would come next and eventually how we would return to being in person. Now, with the pandemic over, many argue we are facing new crises that have emerged as a result. At the forefront are issues of chronic absenteeism, increased mental health needs of students and staff, and learning deficits of students who have fallen behind. Superintendents are rising to these challenges and working with their communities to find creative solutions.

TRAINED BUT NOT PREPARED:
"I didn't take this class in college."

Virtually every superintendent preparation or certification program includes a class or module on communications, often with a strand on crisis communications. There are also hundreds of books and articles on leading through crises and the attributes of effective crisis leadership. Leaders know that clear communication, decisiveness, empathy, adaptability, and collaboration are essential during a crisis, and in the weeks leading up to school closures, superintendents did what they were trained to do. They began strategizing with their teams to prepare logistically, often working seven days a week, beginning early in the morning and going late into the evening. It soon became clear, though, that in many ways they were flying blind. They were using strategies that had worked in the past for familiar crises, but they were now faced with a wholly unfamiliar set of circumstances. The pandemic required superintendents to exercise skills that they were learning in the moment. Their professional preparation had not prepared them for this.

Leading in a crisis always involves balancing immediate and long-term needs and priorities, but all of the unknowns during the pandemic made achieving that balance incredibly difficult. Managing information and emotions on a daily basis was challenging, and planning for the inevitable return to school increased that pressure significantly. With no set guidelines to follow, district leaders had to scramble to make decisions that met the needs of their communities. What worked in one district might not be as effective in another. It also seemed that whatever direction superintendents took, there would be criticism. For example, in the case of Matt Miller, former superintendent in the Lakota School District in Ohio, once he knew that his district would be sending students and staff home for remote learning, he cancelled classes early to do a "dry run" with his staff to ensure they were prepared:

> We made sure all of our devices were deployed, and I actually called school off on the Friday before the shutdown because I wanted to have a practice dry run of 1:1 devices with teachers and students. At the time the [reaction from staff and families] was a little mixed, because some were [critical], saying, "Oh, we are going to be back in three weeks, so you are kind of overreacting." But it was probably one of the better decisions we made.

Miller was hardly alone in facing criticism around his decision.

A few states away in Virginia, Dr. Gregory Hutchings, former superintendent of Alexandria City Public Schools, was facing pushback for making the opposite decision. He kept his schools open two days after all others in the state had closed so he could ensure that every student went home with a working computer:

> Every school system in our area closed on that Wednesday, and I chose to close on Friday. I got a lot of flak because [people were saying] "Everyone else is closed. It's a world disaster. People are dying." So, I really had to talk the board into us staying open for those two extra days. . . . We worked literally 48 hours straight and I got zero sleep, but it was the best decision we ever made because we were the only district in Virginia where every student had a computer during the pandemic.

These two examples illustrate what was part of most superintendents' reality during the pandemic: they were damned if they did, and damned if they didn't. Many times, there were no good answers to be found, and we had to land on the least bad one, which, to no one's surprise, was not well-received by our staff, students, and communities. All too often, the available options made for a no-win situation.

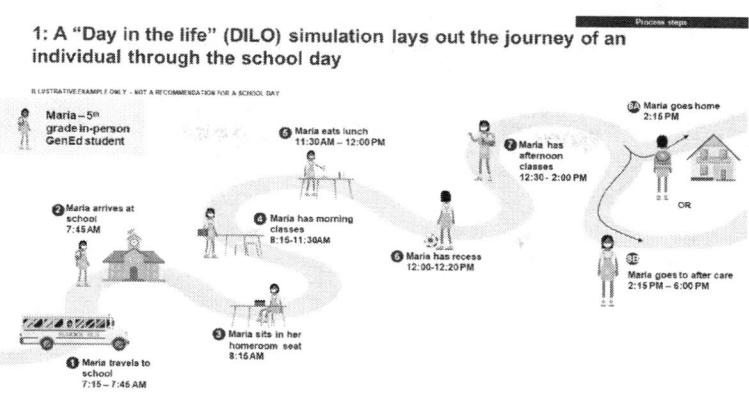

Figure 1.2. Examples of DILO resources describing some of the considerations for a return to in-person learning. *Source*: Chiefs for Change and Council of Chief State School Officers.

Fortunately, school districts were not alone in figuring out ways to navigate these troubling realities. Many national and state organizations and professional associations, in addition to the Centers for Disease Control, issued guidance in an effort to assist school districts in their decision-making. Two of these groups, Chiefs for Change and the Council of Chief State School Officers, teamed up to support Highline Public Schools and Broward County Public Schools in developing "A Day in the Life of (DILO)" simulation tools.[2] Figures 1.2 and 1.3 provide examples. During the simulation process, superintendents and members of their leadership teams came together for two- to four-hour sessions where they would walk through every detailed step needed in determining how to bring students and staff back to school. Depending on the particular questions or issues that arose, they also engaged with families, teachers, and community members.

For example, once schools reopened, districts had to have a plan in place for what to do if a student began exhibiting COVID-19 symptoms during the school day. Where would the student be isolated in the school to prevent further exposure, particularly if a family member could not arrive for pick-up right away? Who would the school need to notify and how? Would "deep cleaning" of the classroom be necessary, or would the district need to close that classroom, or even the school, temporarily? And how would the communication process ensure the health and safety of the school community while also protecting the student's privacy?

Answering these questions, while also continuing to provide instruction and emotional support, would prove to be a tall order. Susan described the

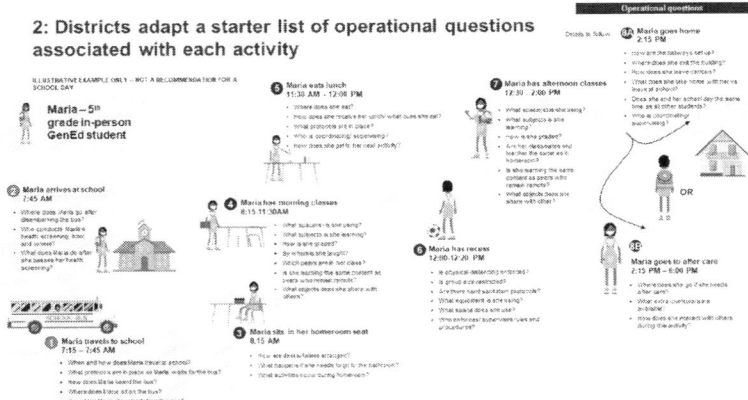

Figure 1.3. Examples of DILO resources describing some of the considerations for a return to in-person learning. *Source*: Chiefs for Change and Council of Chief State School Officers.

painstaking process her team went through, like so many other district teams across the country:

> Our team never worked as hard as they did from March through June of 2020. Not only were we having to establish ways to make remote learning work, but we also had to plan for the safe return to school buildings, and that involved a level of detail we had never before encountered. We literally mapped it out minute-by-minute, from the time students left their homes to get on a bus to travel to school, to when they entered the building and had to be screened. It was exhausting and felt never-ending at times.

While resources like DILO may not have been equally applicable to all districts, having access to such simulation tools was helpful to many. It spared superintendents and their teams from having to attempt to create something similar on their own.

KNOWING WHAT TO COMMUNICATE AND WHEN:
"We had to learn responsible transparency."

Superintendents have always understood the need for agility and flexibility, but these qualities took on whole new meanings during the pandemic, with so many unknowns and such an overwhelming volume of information that needed to be reviewed and communicated. The ability to pivot quickly often proved challenging for those of us who prided ourselves on being structured and intentional leaders. Hutchings summed up how these changed circumstances pushed him out of his leadership comfort zone:

> Prior to the pandemic I was very structured. Like, if this is what we're going to do, we're going to do it! I always had some flexibility, but I was always [clear that] this is our mission, this is what we're striving for. So my having to pivot like that was a huge change for my leadership and a challenge.

Similarly, Dr. Alan Spicciati, Auburn School District superintendent, found himself challenged as a leader to be the "Communicator-in-Chief," a role with which he was not entirely comfortable:

> It made me much more aware of the importance of [my] role as a community leader, as a leader of other educators. I've [always] taken a lower profile approach to communications. I really want parents to have their primary relationship to be with the principal of the school. But in the pandemic that's not what our community needed. They needed to hear from me.

The experiences of these two leaders illustrate what so many superintendents faced. They were accustomed to having the answers and a strategy in place for whatever challenge arose. Now they found themselves having to make sense of information that was constantly shifting, determine what to communicate and when, and change course with little warning or preparation.

Clear, consistent communication is an integral part of leadership, and in a crisis, it becomes indispensable. In early 2020, superintendents had to effectively convey information and manage misinformation and disinformation while also maintaining trust within their communities. There was often significant pressure from staff and families to provide information when it would have been premature and irresponsible to do so—superintendents knew they had to be as right as they could, as often as they could.

Superintendents had to learn to work closely with public health officials and other leaders in their communities to disseminate information as it evolved. They knew the importance of providing regular updates and being as transparent as possible. Still, there were limitations to that transparency. As Dr. Baron Davis, former superintendent in Richland School District Two in South Carolina, described it, "we had to learn responsible transparency. Everyone can't know everything at the same time, particularly when things are unknown. [We had to] be able to respond quickly when needed but also know when we didn't need to respond quickly." He illustrated this point by describing his district's decision-making process for determining what infection-rate threshold would trigger the school to move from in-person learning to hybrid or remote:

Initially, we considered closing schools if the local infection rate exceeded five percent. However, new guidelines suggested a more nuanced approach, allowing schools to stay open with strict protocols if rates were between five percent and seven percent. Had we shared that initial threshold widely, families and staff might have panicked when local rates approached five percent, expecting an imminent shutdown, which could have caused disruption and anxiety. Sharing every change in criteria could have led to confusion and a lack of trust, as stakeholders might have felt decisions were inconsistent or arbitrary. Instead, it was best to wait until we had a clear, actionable plan based on the most current guidelines and data. We then communicated this final decision with clear justifications and instructions, minimizing confusion and anxiety. By carefully managing information dissemination, we ensured that stakeholders received relevant, clear, and accurate information tailored to their needs and responsibilities, thus maintaining trust and stability during a highly volatile time.

In other words, there were times when less was certainly more, and COVID-19 presented superintendents with many of those times.

It was not just the pressure of preventing unnecessary alarm; it was also the weight superintendents carried, knowing that they were sometimes making potentially life-and-death decisions. Dr. Scott Muri, former superintendent of Ector County Independent School District in Texas, described the heaviness of this responsibility:

Early on we were talking about the number of deaths that could occur in Texas. And these were all projections, but just having that information as a leader, knowing this large number of casualties was potentially very real, and every decision that I made might impact it in one way or another [was a lot]. It was far beyond academics, it was human life. Whom do you debrief that with? You don't want to scare your family or your team.

Superintendents felt this burden acutely, especially since what was understood to be accurate today could likely change tomorrow.

In times of crisis, making swift and informed decisions is essential. Evaluating risks, anticipating needs, and taking action in the moment, however, can be emotional. During the pandemic, when fear and uncertainty ran rampant in their communities, superintendents had to project confidence and calm while also exhibiting honesty and vulnerability. As Hutchings said,

You're not taught to be vulnerable as a leader, but I think tapping into my vulnerability helped me be a better leader during the crisis because I had to be honest and say, "you know, I don't have the answer for that."

SUPERINTENDENTS ARE PEOPLE FIRST:
"I was crying off camera."

Being the face of the district was nothing new, but being that face during the pandemic made superintendents a target at times. Some in their communities wanted someone to blame, a focus for their anger, fear, and frustration. Superintendents were often on the receiving end of barrages of harsh sentiments. Hutchings's experience was hardly unique as he described the wave of criticism he received in response to his decision-making: "I was getting the worst emails of how stupid I was, and how crazy I am, and I'm going to kill all these people . . . that my blood, their blood, is going to be on my hands." While hyperbolic, the accusations nevertheless had their intended effect: superintendents felt hurt and attacked. The emotional toll of being the leader and chief messenger during this time was very real.

The backlash that some experienced could also be frightening and extreme. In some parts of the country, the decision to return students and staff to their school buildings was incredibly contentious. In the Seattle area, tremendous pushback erupted from some staff and families when it came time to discuss reopening. The resistance that superintendents faced proved difficult to manage. It required demonstrating both empathy and concern for people's well-being, along with mission-driven decisiveness to educate children.

Despite having every health mitigation strategy in place, staff and families wanted guarantees that superintendents simply could not in good conscience provide. They could do everything within their power to mitigate the risks of exposure, but they could not guarantee that people would not get sick. Some districts, like Highline in the Puget Sound, had to take legal action to get staff back into schools, filing injunctions requiring them to return.[3] Superintendents were called names and at times even threatened. One such instance occurred in April 2021, when Highline's central office was vandalized with the words "Racist Superintendent" spray painted across its entrance as illustrated in figure 1.4. Sadly, this was not an isolated event, as too many district leaders across the country faced similar threats and attacks that impacted them professionally and personally.

Dr. David Schuler, executive director of the American Association of School Administrators (AASA) and former superintendent of Township High School District 214 in Illinois, provided a particularly poignant example of what it means to "lead now and feel later" when he described suffering the loss of a beloved staff member but having to stay strong to help one of his principals get through it:

> Your job is to lead, not to feel at that point. I got a call from a principal and he said, "Dave, one of our security guards just died and is outside in the student

Figure 1.4. Vandalized entrance to Highline Public Schools Central Office from 2021. Source: Photograph courtesy of Tove Tupper.

parking lot. What should I do?" So I walked him through exactly the steps we were going to take, and he called me back the next day and asked, "How were you so calm throughout all of that?" And I said, "That's my job. I knew her, I loved her, I respected her. I will grieve later. My job was to help you lead through that situation [in that moment]."

In many ways, the pandemic highlighted superintendents at their best: modeling strength and vulnerability, communicating hope and reassurance, demonstrating empathy and courage, and ultimately keeping students at the center of their decision-making.

Many superintendents have been candid about the personal toll that leading through the pandemic and navigating so many unknowns took on them, and in some cases, on their families. In spite of the stress and criticism, however, all the superintendents we have interviewed remain grateful and honored to have served their communities during such a trying time.

EXEMPLARY LEADERSHIP: DR. ALAN SPICCIATI ON THE IMPORTANCE OF HOPE AND OPTIMISM

Spicciati has served as the superintendent for the Auburn School District (ASD) in Washington state since 2015. The district encompasses a 62-mile area bridging King and Pierce counties and "is committed to fulfilling its mission of providing [its] 17,000 students with an education that [will] engage, educate, and empower each student for success beyond graduation." ASD has three comprehensive high schools, one alternative high school, four middle schools, and sixteen elementary schools. They also house early learning programs at their elementary schools and offer life skills training for students ages 18–21 in a Transition Assistance Program. ASD is richly diverse, with 33 percent of its student population identifying as Hispanic. In addition, approximately 25 percent of students are English learners, 12 percent receive special education support, and 63 percent of students qualify for free or reduced lunch.

In the fall of 2019, Spicciati was beginning his fifth year leading ASD and was feeling good about the direction of the district. Like most new superintendents, he had spent his first few years building relationships with staff and the community, hiring a strong, dedicated team, and developing a strategic plan to guide the district in its mission to engage and educate every student. He had faced challenges and crises over those years, but none had prepared him for what would come in March 2020.

Spicciati, along with other superintendents in his region, had been carefully following the progression of the virus and the chatter that was beginning to arise around potential school closures. Because of this early tracking, they had some preparations in place once the decision was made to send students home for at least six to eight weeks on March 13, 2020. Like districts around the state and country, they mobilized to distribute devices and meals and organized food drives for families, while also transitioning teaching and learning from in-person to remote. It soon became clear to him, however, that these logistical decisions were nothing compared to the decisions he would soon find himself making to ensure the health and safety of his staff, students, and families:

> I remember a moment where it hit me viscerally that the decisions I made could have life or death consequences. I was working late one night in the days before the closure decision, and our admin building custodian came in to talk about if she should retire. She was older and was learning that she was at high risk for a bad outcome from COVID-19. For some reason, that was the point it really hit me. Here is the sweetest person, who has been nothing but loyal to me and the school district. It was weighty to realize the decisions we made could be life or death for her. And then you think, it's not just her, it's other older staff, immunocompromised staff, and medically fragile family members of staff and students. I was alone in my office. It was a very somber moment pondering the consequences. I was used to making big decisions, difficult decisions, but this had a different weight to it.

Like other superintendents, Spicciati found himself struggling to stay focused on the day-to-day decisions required to keep learning going while school buildings were closed—when the reality was that members of his community were getting sick and dying from COVID-19. Some days required him to show up as best he could, despite what he was feeling. This struggle was compounded by sentiments in his community that were beginning to feel overwhelmingly negative, as Spicciati recalled:

> In July of 2020, I went to a graduation party for two students I knew. It was outdoors, COVID-19 rates had stabilized, and we were keeping a distance. These were kids who played baseball with my son, and I knew the other parents there well. One guy came up to me and said, "I wouldn't want your job right now." I know he meant well, but it had a hopeless tone to it. Shortly after, another friend made a similar comment. It started to feel like a pity party. I decided I needed to do something. When a third person said I was in a tough position, with an upbeat tone and a smile I confidently replied, "We're making the best of it." That single statement changed the weather in the room. It acknowledged the challenge, but reframed it as can-do.

What became a hallmark of Spicciati's leadership during this time was his commitment to remaining positive while also understanding the critical role he played as a leader in maintaining hope within his community:

> I came up with a mantra of hope, optimism, and problem-solving. I said, hope, optimism, and problem-solving probably eight hundred times, in every public speech and in writing and all those things. And if it was informal, I stuck with the "we're going to make the best of it" [line]. But we had so many people who would fixate on the challenges and disappointments, and [I] really had to reframe that. . . . That's where the problem-solving came in.

His expressions of steady confidence, hope, and optimism helped his community to follow his lead and know that, as impossible as it felt, they would make it through this time.

One of his greatest points of pride, and an excellent example of the creative problem-solving by superintendents, was ASD's Elementary PM program. In preparing for the 2020–2021 school year, which would begin with all students learning full-time from home, Spicciati and his team surveyed families and learned that a surprising number of them, elementary families in particular, wanted an evening school option for their children given the challenges they were encountering in conducting school from home, as illustrated in figure 1.5:

> [Many] families couldn't be around to help their children during normal school hours because they were working. Or the kids stayed with grandma during the

Figure 1.5. An Auburn School District family gathered in their bathroom for remote learning. *Source*: Photograph courtesy of the Kari family.

day, and she didn't have internet access. There were many stories, but the common thread was these were our least advantaged families with parents barely making ends meet. Three weeks before school started, we pulled the trigger on what we called the Elementary PM [or evening] Program. It was scary. This felt like a huge risk. But it was so rewarding. School started in the mid-afternoon with enrichment programming, since some parents wouldn't be home. Reading was before dinner and math after, as these were the prime times. We always took a dinner break. And the PM program finished at 8 p.m. with teachers reading stories to the whole family. This was such a huge equity move. Ultimately, we had four hundred students enrolled for the year, and the Elementary PM Program became our most diverse, low-income school.

He went on to describe the story of one mother who cleaned hotel rooms at night and had to take her young son with her so he had a safe environment with reliable internet access—and where the hotel staff even helped him with his homework at times. In Spicciati's words, "it moved me to tears." While his strength and empathy were exceptional, he would be the first to say that he is hardly an exception; superintendents everywhere have similar stories. There is, however, no question that Spicciati exemplified superintendent pandemic leadership at its best.

INSIGHTS AND TAKEAWAYS FROM NAVIGATING THE UNKNOWN

- *Find strength in vulnerability.* As much pressure as leaders put on themselves to have all the answers, and as much as their communities expect them to, the reality is they sometimes do not. Rather than fake it, or become defensive, superintendents learned to lean in and admit to the public when they did not know something, or when they made a mistake. Being vulnerable in this way can be uncomfortable, but in the end it is a sign of strength, not weakness. It also strengthens the trust and confidence which the community has in its leadership.
- *Be nimble.* As Dr. Kristine Gilmore, former superintendent of D.C. Everest Area School District, Wisconsin, said, "We now know schools are not the *Titanic*. We used to think we couldn't move [our school systems], but we became very nimble, very quickly." While the ability to adjust and adapt has always been important, it became part of superintendents' daily lives, so much so that today we know we can and must move more quickly to do right by our students, staff, and families. Educators are far less likely today to allow the phrase "This is how we have always done it" to be sufficient justification for not making necessary changes.
- *Lead from your values.* During the pandemic, superintendents' decisions were questioned, but so were their values. When staff or families did not agree with a decision, they would sometimes accuse superintendents of not caring about them. When challenged in this way, it was imperative to know where they stood and why they stood there. Communicating the values that drive decision-making is essential.

Navigating the unknowns that came with the pandemic pushed superintendents in ways that challenged them both personally and professionally. They had to rely on their training, their colleagues, and their values—in addition to guidance from state and federal officials—to chart a path forward for their communities. Looking back, many see things they would have done differently, but in that moment, they gave their very best.

NOTES

1. Gemma D'Auria and Aaron De Smet, "Leadership in a Crisis: Responding to the Coronavirus Outbreak and Future Challenges," March 16, 2020, https://www.mckinsey.com/capabilities/people-and-organizational-performance/our-insights/leadership-in-a-crisis-responding-to-the-coronavirus-outbreak-and-future-challenges.

2. Chiefs for Change and Council of Chief State School Officers, "Day in the Life of (DILO) Resources," July 2020, https://chiefsforchange.org/wp-content/uploads/2020/08/200801-1000-DILO-simulation-and-resources.pdf.

3. Highline Public Schools did file an injunction in the spring of 2021, during negotiations with union leadership, to return to in-person learning, but the day before they were scheduled to appear in court, they reached an agreement.

Chapter 2

Connecting through the Power of Networking

I wouldn't be a superintendent if it wasn't for the support of the "Sister Supes."

—Superintendent Heidi Sipe,
Umatilla School District, Oregon

Networking became as much a part of the COVID-19 experience as isolation was, with the two phenomena inextricably linked. As the virus spread, long-established ways of gathering to exchange information and confer with colleagues were abruptly halted. For superintendents and others in roles of leadership and responsibility, in-person meetings became rare or stopped altogether. Meanwhile, the crisis made sharing ideas, experiences, and innovations more essential than ever. So, parallel to classroom education going remote or hybrid, the work of superintendents also moved to virtual platforms. With the help of technology, superintendents connected with peers from other districts, attended distant conferences remotely, and participated in online professional learning communities. In the uncharted territory of COVID-19, such dedicated, tech-assisted networking proved that "we're in this together" is a far better place to be than alone on one's own.

Networking—being part of an active set of formal and informal connections within the field—was and is a crucial strategy for superintendents. During the COVID-19 pandemic, they leaned on these connections to provide support, resources, ideas, and opportunities for collaboration. Ultimately, this collaboration enabled superintendents to navigate pandemic-era challenges more successfully.

An enduring legacy of the pandemic, increased networking, is still with us. It continues to contribute to the professional growth of superintendents and the operational success of their school districts. Superintendents use it to share best practices and engage in collaborative problem-solving. The technological advances that occurred during COVID-19 make it easier for superintendents, and everyone, to reach out and connect with other people, known and unknown. Just as important, the value of the relationships forged during the pandemic has led some superintendents to form affinity groups to support other post-pandemic efforts. These groups provide collegial sounding boards and ready access to others who are dealing with similar issues. Then and now, networking often plays a key role in doing a difficult job well.

NO "ONE-SIZE-FITS-ALL" NETWORKING:
"I relied heavily on my networks to survive."

When asked about what it was like learning of possible school closures in the district early in the pandemic, Superintendent Dr. Heidi Sipe, who leads a small rural school district in Oregon, had two words: "wild time." Like many in her position, she thought they would be closed for only a two-week pause in March of 2020. At the time, their district was in great shape when it came to the ability to respond and quickly communicate, so initially the break did not seem of enormous consequence. Soon, her perspective shifted. The pause went from being one of the superintendent's "favorite times" in her career to one of the most demanding. What helped get her through it? The support and camaraderie found in a weekly informal group meeting called the "Sister Supes."

Some superintendents felt, however, that they did not have the time to take advantage of formal or informal networking opportunities. They would communicate only with their immediate team to address the multitude of specific issues facing them. Superintendent Dr. Mary Elizabeth Davis of Cherokee County School District, Georgia, said it was not unusual for her and her executive team to meet from 6 a.m. until 10 p.m. each day during those first few months of COVID-19. They spent hours deciphering the changing protocols and guidelines from state officials, leaving little time to meet with anyone else.

State associations for school administrators offered weekly platforms for superintendents to meet and share decisions regarding such issues as reopening and mitigation guidelines and quarantine requirements coming from public health officials. Nevertheless, during the pandemic, the consistency in guidance from state officials varied, with recommendations sometimes rapidly changing. In some states, decisions were left to superintendents to make—about when to reopen schools, whether to require masks in schools, if schools would or would not require vaccinations of employees, and how to answer other tough questions that arose related to the pandemic.

During many of the state-level meetings, the agendas were about disseminating guidance around COVID-19-related issues. Thinking back, Davis reported that since there was not time in those meetings to discuss the impact of COVID-19 on their own health and wellness, they relied instead on existing professional relationships, such as with other superintendents in their state, region, or elsewhere, to focus on health and wellness support for each other.

Whether superintendents became part of wider virtual groups, talked informally with friends and colleagues, or conferred only with inner-circle team members due to time constraints, networking during COVID-19 proved irreplaceable. There was no one way to network, but consensus emerged that the effectiveness of superintendents in fostering educational excellence and systemic improvements significantly hinges on their ability to leverage both informal and formal networks. These networks provide resources, support, and collaborative opportunities that enhance decision-making, leadership skills, and overall school district performance.

To better serve students, superintendents made innovative use of their networks within their communities during the pandemic. Dr. David Schuler, former superintendent of Township High School District 214, said his district team provided hot spots to students, but his team knew the speed of access differed from one location to another and within homes. In recognition of that varying level of broadband speed, they partnered with local municipalities to run their school internet services from schools to mobile homes and libraries. They also were able to bounce the internet feed off water towers, enabling faster service to students.

In essence, where a student had a device, the district's goal was to ensure the student was receiving the same level of internet speed as if they were in school. In fulfilling these responsibilities, superintendents navigated complex administrative, pedagogical, technological, and community-oriented tasks. During this complex and ever-changing time, superintendents harnessed knowledge from both formal and informal networks to find solutions for the challenges facing their communities.

BUILDING RELATIONSHIPS THROUGH INFORMAL NETWORKS:
"We will be forever bonded."

Informal networks consist of personal connections and relationships that superintendents develop over time. These networks often include peers, mentors, colleagues, and community members with whom superintendents share trust and mutual respect. Informal networks are characterized by their fluidity, flexibility, and often spontaneous nature. They provide a platform for candid discussions, peer support, and the sharing of tacit knowledge and experiences that are not typically available through formal channels. For instance, during the sudden outbreak of COVID-19, many superintendents relied on informal networks to gather real-time information, implement best practices, and solicit support from peers, enabling them to respond swiftly and effectively. Informal networks facilitate this exchange of tacit knowledge—the unwritten, experiential knowledge that is often critical for effective leadership.

Informal networks also provide superintendents with emotional support and mentorship, which strengthens their sense of well-being and professional resilience. Through relationships with trusted peers and mentors, superintendents can share challenges and get advice on effective leadership strategies. These connections offer a safe space for superintendents to discuss sensitive issues, receive constructive feedback, and develop a sense of camaraderie.

For example, a new superintendent might face difficulties in managing board relations or implementing a controversial policy. By turning to a mentor within their informal network, they can gain perspectives on navigating these challenges, drawing from the mentor's own experiences and wisdom. During COVID-19, many superintendents formed informal groups to discuss the challenges they were facing, but they also used the opportunity to find commonality, seek consistency, and work together to develop solutions that prioritized the well-being of students and communities.

What types of multifaceted topics arose for superintendents in the COVID-19 crisis and were discussed in informal networking groups? The need for students' food security, improved academic services, and mental health support were three critical concerns. Superintendents were left to decide how to manage these issues for their communities during much, if not all, of the COVID-19 pandemic.

During some of the most challenging times, the relationships and bonds that developed through informal networks showed the effectiveness of collaborative problem-solving. The result was not only enduring partnerships with substantial advantages for students but also an ongoing platform for leaders, providing mutual support.

When asked how the weekly Zoom meetings impacted her relationships with other superintendents, Davis responded that the impact had been profoundly positive:

> There are times today, because of the connections and bonds formed during the pandemic, I can look at a superintendent I met with during weekly Zoom meetings and—because we shared the same value system—know we will forever be bonded differently. It felt supportive during the pandemic to turn to a trusted

group of colleagues, get feedback on ideas, and maintain a level of consistency in decision-making.

She further emphasized that having a trusted group of colleagues during this time was critical.

In addition to fostering beneficial bonds, informal networks provide the time and space for rapid problem-solving and decision-making, essential during the pandemic. Dr. Melvin Brown, who led Reynoldsburg City Schools in Ohio during COVID-19 and currently serves as superintendent for Montgomery Public Schools in Alabama, noted that he talked to at least one superintendent every single day through Zoom, text, or phone calls, and he keeps in touch with many of these superintendents even today.

He was also part of a small group of male superintendents who met in 2020 at an American Association of School Administrators (AASA) networking event and determined that it would be good for them to continue gathering informally. As the COVID-19 crisis stretched out, the group agreed to meet every Friday evening via Zoom to see how each other was doing. Brown said, "The group decided we needed to meet weekly. It really was a way to check in with each other more often because meeting formally at AASA events wasn't good enough." The group has continued meeting at subsequent formal AASA meetings in person to converse, catch up with one another, and compare notes.

DISTRICT TEAMS AS NETWORKS:
"It is really about the commitment."

COVID-19 era communications issues and pressures highlight the role of the superintendent's executive team as a powerful network in and of itself. Davis's biggest lesson learned is that effective teams get results:

> I thought that having a highly effective team was a nice to have and that it helps to attract quality leaders to your district. But what I really learned is that the strength and potential of the district is on the backs of your executive team. Minute by minute as decisions are made, it is really about the commitment to each other to figure out the work.

She saw how this approach could be applied more generally, adding, "We have created an internal culture that sustains effectiveness throughout times of crisis and allows for our district to effectively manage, regardless of the crisis we may be facing."

Like districts everywhere, Davis's former district had faced a range of critical incidents, such as cybersecurity attacks and violence involving guns and other weapons on campuses. She commented on how dealing with adversity in positive, effective, and capable ways can strengthen bonds—bonds that can then be well-established and in place when they are needed in the future:

> We aren't numb to crisis nor does a crisis merely stop. But the idea that you can have a culture that is built to excel when crisis occurs—and you have gained the trust and confidence of your community in your ability to handle the crisis—speaks to the lessons learned and strategies applied during the pandemic.

The superintendents we interviewed all identified the need for agility and noted they can learn from each other's successes and failures, gaining practical insights that are not readily available in formal training programs. Dr. Heidi Sipe, superintendent of Umatilla School District, Oregon, shared a powerful example of connection that occurred during COVID-19. She recalled a time when the group Sister Supes, the networking group she relied on most, met and learned how each superintendent was dealing with the grief and emotions felt across schools regarding George Floyd's murder, which occurred on May 25, 2020, in Minneapolis, and regarding the Black Lives Matter movement. She reported seeing another side of people whom she admired in leadership roles, as each expressed their own vulnerability and humility. The takeaway here is that stresses and challenges often remain the same for superintendents, regardless of where they serve.

COMBATING ISOLATION:
"Only a lonely job if you allow it to be."

Having a group of trusted colleagues in troubled times provides necessary support to superintendents to sustain the strength to carry on. These colleagues support each other in finding ways to balance the demands of the job, take care of their own health and wellness, and deal with crises and trauma that may arise. Schuler captured this idea powerfully:

> I lost years of my life during the pandemic, sitting in the chair of the superintendent, and yet there is no place I would have rather been to have the opportunity to help lead my students and community during that time. It's something I will honor and cherish forever. I came to rely on the weekly informal Zoom meeting that consisted of three superintendents, one each from the east and west coast and one CEO. The group represented red, blue, and purple states politically, and purposely met to check in on each other but also to review changing guidelines.

Schuler believes that such COVID-19-related guidelines were critical for superintendents to remain successful.

Networking provided an overview of how the guidance would affect decisions impacting the overall operations of schools. Seeing value in getting multiple perspectives, Schuler made the following observation, now in his new role as executive director of the AASA:

> Being a superintendent is only a lonely job if you allow it to be. The networks both formal and informal—the connections and relationships that are built while you are superintendent—are critical to your success. It's imperative that superintendents find communities of practice that can help all of us to implement better programs and ultimately policies leading to better student outcomes. We don't have to all implement the same things, but we should at least understand what people are thinking, what school boards are doing, and what steps are being taken to implement things.

In Schuler's view, understanding what steps colleagues are considering and taking is of vital importance in doing a good job. As he put it, those steps were the "things we discussed during weekly meetings that helped us the most during the pandemic."

Informal networks are instrumental in building trust and fostering collaboration among superintendents. The human element of these networks promotes a culture of mutual support and shared problem-solving. Superintendents who surround themselves with trusted colleagues are more likely to collaborate on initiatives, share resources, work together to address common challenges, and resist isolation.

THE INFLUENCE OF FORMAL NETWORKS:
"Networking gave me perspective."

Formal networks are structured and institutionalized. They include professional associations, educational consortia, governmental bodies, and other organized groups that superintendents join as part of their professional development and leadership roles. Formal networks offer access to standardized resources, professional training, policy updates, and collaborative initiatives. They are essential for staying informed about the latest educational trends, policies, and best practices. For superintendents, formal networks offer structured opportunities for professional development, enhancement of leadership skills, and the latest updates on educational trends and policies. Through workshops, conferences, and training programs, formal networks provide superintendents with the knowledge and tools to lead their districts effectively. Dr. Joe Gothard, former superintendent of St. Paul Public Schools, Minnesota, and currently superintendent of Madison Metropolitan School

District, Wisconsin, reflected on his involvement with the Council of the Great City Schools:

> Bringing together other like districts was important to me. It wasn't so much that I had that much in common with the other districts, it was the perspective it gave me. And I always left those calls feeling very humbled.

Other organizations, like AASA, offer a range of professional development programs tailored to superintendents and their districts. These programs cover instructional leadership, financial management, community engagement, and other topics designed to equip superintendents with the competencies required for their roles.

There is another advantage to formal networks: they provide access to standardized resources, research, and best practices that superintendents can implement in their districts. These resources are often developed by educational experts based on rigorous research, ensuring their reliability and effectiveness. A superintendent seeking to improve literacy rates in their district can turn to formal networks for evidence-based strategies and programs that have been proven to work in similar contexts. For example, AASA's Early Learning Cohort provides support for superintendents and their district teams regarding literacy and early learning.[1]

By adopting the best practices learned through a formal network like the AASA Early Learning Cohort, the superintendent can enhance instructional quality and student outcomes.

Using reliable research and in-depth knowledge associated with respected formal networks, affiliated superintendents can better interact with lawmakers and shape relevant policy. Superintendents do indeed engage in policy advocacy and influence educational policy at the local, state, and national levels. By participating in formal organizations, superintendents can collaborate with their peers to advocate for policies that support public education and address the issues of their districts. For instance, through membership in state superintendent associations, superintendents can collectively voice their recommendations to policymakers, shaping legislation that impacts funding, accountability, and educational standards. The recommendations for increased funding to close the achievement gap—recommendations based on lessons learned during the pandemic—will be powerful coming from superintendents.

Finally, formal networks foster collaboration and innovation by bringing together superintendents from diverse backgrounds and contexts. These networks create platforms for sharing innovative practices, conducting joint research, and developing collaborative projects that drive educational improvement. A superintendent involved in a formal network focused on STEM (Science, Technology, Engineering, and Mathematics) education might collaborate with peers to design and implement innovative STEM programs across multiple districts, leveraging collective expertise and resources to achieve greater impact.

A Combination Greater Than the Sum of Its Parts: "The challenge always is to make time."For superintendents, the true power of networking lies in the synergy between informal and formal networks. Combining both types confers benefits greater than one or the other alone. By accessing both types of networks, superintendents can create a robust support system that enhances their leadership effectiveness and drives systemic improvement. They can build a comprehensive support system that addresses their diverse needs. Informal networks provide the relational and emotional support necessary for personal and professional resilience, while formal networks offer access to structured resources, training, and policy influence. A superintendent who actively engages in both types of networks is better equipped to navigate the complexities of their role, contributing to and drawing on a wide range of support and expertise.

Similarly, the combination of informal and formal networks enhances superintendents' decision-making capabilities. Informal networks offer real-time experiential knowledge, while formal networks provide access to research-based evidence and best practices. This dual approach enables superintendents to make informed, balanced decisions that consider both practical experiences and empirical data. For example, when implementing a new instructional program, a superintendent can have informal conversations with peers who have piloted similar programs, alongside formal research and guidelines from professional organizations to ensure a successful rollout.

Engaging in both informal and formal networks means that superintendents learn from a broader range of perspectives and ideas, fostering innovation and creativity. Informal networks often introduce superintendents to unconventional approaches and grassroots innovations, while formal networks provide exposure to cutting-edge research and policy trends. Superintendents participating in a formal network's conference might learn about new educational technology, which they can then discuss with peers in their informal networks to explore practical applications and potential challenges before implementation.

Superintendents can use their networking skills to strengthen relationships with community members and stakeholders. Informal networks form a way for superintendents to build personal connections with community leaders, parents, and local organizations, fostering trust and collaboration. Formal networks, meanwhile, provide a platform for engaging with policymakers, business leaders, and educational experts. A superintendent who maintains strong informal ties with local community leaders and actively participates in formal policy advocacy groups can effectively bridge the gap between community realities and policy initiatives. Doing so will ensure that their district's interests are well represented and supported.

EXEMPLARY LEADERSHIP: DR. A. KATRISE LEE-PERERA ON SISTER SUPES

During the pandemic, Dr. A. Katrise Lee-Perera was serving as superintendent for the Gresham-Barlow School District in Oregon, a midsized urban district. Her experience exemplifies the power of combining informal and formal networks. Wanting to create a space for colleagues to meet, Lee-Perera sought support from both her informal network of trusted peers and her formal network of professional associations during COVID-19. Reflecting on those challenging times, she said, "I remember feeling the isolation and weight of decisions on me, not having anyone to understand the plight because they weren't in the position. In my need for some help with my mental health, for selfish reasons I called a group of female leaders I knew from near and far and formed the Sister Supes."

Through informal conversations that resulted, Lee-Perera learned about peers' successes with COVID-19 but also learned the power of collaboration. She started Sister Supes as a way for women superintendents to stay connected during COVID-19 and to talk about issues they were facing both personally and professionally. In 2020, AASA released its Decennial Study of Superintendents. The percentage of superintendents who are women increased slightly from 2010, when it was 24.1 percent, to 26.7 percent in 2020. The findings in the 2020 study were based on survey answers from 1,218 superintendents across the country. Given that the nation's public school superintendents represent about 13,000 public schools, it can be inferred that the survey was somewhat limited in scope. However, it seems safe to say that only about one in four school superintendents is female, so creating safe places to meet and support one another became invaluable during the pandemic. The scheduled weekly Zoom meetings began in March of 2020, and the bonds formed during COVID-19 will last forever.

Week-to-week, the group considered many urgent topics within the profession, including contact tracing, masking, and protocols for reopening schools. Sometimes they would talk about what Lee-Perera describes as digital exclusivity—that is, working through creative ways to solve the problem of getting kids access to internet connectivity. Other times, the group would discuss the rapid shift in teaching and learning and would listen to how different colleagues were handling the changes themselves, how teachers and teams were responding, and what tools they were using to address the challenges.

Even more important than the discussion of specific topics was the support these women provided one another, which was Lee-Perera's motivation for starting Sister Supes in the beginning. Due to the tremendous stress on school communities, on families, and on the superintendents themselves, having a space to talk contributed greatly to their success and well-being. As seen in figure 2.1, it shows one of the many times that Sister Supes met during COVID-19 on a Sunday afternoon during the pandemic.

As noted earlier, Sipe said, in referring back to a time of particular intensity, "We covered such delicate and heartbreaking issues such as George Floyd's murder and leaned on each other's experiences and vulnerabilities." These conversations assisted those involved, she continued, "to discover strategies to mitigate the isolation brought on by the pandemic." In turn, each superintendent who participated in the Sister Supes group has said the concepts, ideas, and thoughts learned throughout the time together have been central to their own personal and professional journeys during COVID-19.

The true power of people coming together, gathering informally to support one another, stands as a lesson learned and applied after the pandemic. The group still checks on each other whenever they meet at professional

Figure 2.1. A Sunday gathering of the Sister Supes during COVID-19. *Source*: Photograph courtesy of Dr. A. Katrise Lee-Perera.

Figure 2.2. The power of connection, as the Sister Supes meet in person during an AASA National Conference on Education in 2023. *Source*: Photograph courtesy of Dr. A. Katrise Lee-Perera.

conferences or events across the country, as illustrated in figure 2.2. The bonds that formed during that time will be long-lasting. Moving forward, a sustaining idea is firmly set, stemming from the Sister Supes experience—namely that, regardless of the size of the district, location, or years of service, oftentimes leaders experience similar stresses and challenges. They willingly support each other and develop strategies and ideas, even after COVID-19 has receded.

Sipe has continued working collaboratively with other superintendents in Oregon. Their goal is to ensure that both informal and formal networks are in place for superintendents in the state and region post-COVID-19. In a formal venue, they are working across state lines to host regional women's conferences to impact leadership, enhance recruitment, and address retention issues. Working with the Confederation of School Administrators in Oregon (COSA), Sipe has also taken lessons from the Sister Supes and reignited a female superintendent group within COSA to meet on a more regular basis. She returned to a previously held monthly meeting style, where potluck-style meals create opportunities to form productive working relationships and encourage the safety and openness to share. Lee-Perera has also formed groups like the "Sister" groups in Texas.

Although the group no longer meets weekly, all are confident that anyone, if asked, would be willing and able to meet virtually at a moment's notice.

And many within it still remain connected today, when the Sister Supes often meet, reflect, and discuss things that are going on professionally and personally in their lives.

Adaptability epitomized educational systems during the pandemic and was a crucial characteristic in successful leadership styles, too. Lee-Perera said, "A reflective leader knows themselves first and can adapt to different types of learning situations if they know themselves."

This thinking can apply to an equitable mindset about access, for example. She explains how difficult it was for students who had a device without broadband to connect to the internet or who had slow internet service to download materials, in comparison to students who were able to access the virtual instruction and curriculum seamlessly. Lee-Perera sees herself as a "student-first" advocate, and her priority to focus on what students need in the moment comes from her ability to lead with an equitable mindset. Leaders who can themselves access opportunities and ideas from groups like the Sister Supes are better able to find support for their students and improve overall outcomes.

When asked what she learned most from the Sister Supes and why it was started, Lee-Perera cut to the heart of the matter and said, "I was running pretty low and needed someone to talk to." It can be hard, long term, to achieve a sustainable balance in a position that can involve (as the COVID-19 years showed) trauma, conflicting constituencies, intractable social ills, and a deluge of cultural, technological, and budget pressures. During COVID-19, thanks to the Sister Supes group, people got to meet and talk on a regular basis with peers who have "been there." They were aided immeasurably by others who are similarly committed to doing a good job at a hard job while maintaining their own health and wellness. In other words, Sister Supes has helped many people to *not run low*.

EXEMPLARY LEADERSHIP: DR. MICHAEL LUBELFELD, DR. NICK POLYAK, TEN YEARS OF SUPT CHAT

At its height, 500 people convened on the first Wednesday of every month with Dr. Mike Lubelfeld, superintendent of Deerfield Public Schools District 109, Illinois, and Dr. Nick Polyak, superintendent of Leyden High School District 212, Illinois, to engage in an informal networking event called Supt Chat. Now, this networking event has celebrated ten years of chats held on social media. The superintendents completed the hundredth Supt Chat in January 2024 and have since retired their authorship of the chat.

Started in October 2014, "#suptchat" formed as a formal subgroup within AASA's certification group, the National Superintendent Certification

Figure 2.3. Superintendents Mike Lubelfeld and Nick Polyak proudly display the "#suptchat" phrase at an AASA National Conference Event. *Source*: Photograph courtesy of Dr. Nick Polyak.

Program. The #suptchat name was coined and established by Dr. Daniel Frazier, former superintendent of Belmond-Klemme Community School District, Iowa, and now assistant professor of Education Leadership at Midwestern State University, Texas. His idea was to make it easy for people to stay connected. While #suptchat has long provided a way for superintendents to learn about the power of messaging, video meetings, social connection via technology, and professional development, it was an especially helpful platform during COVID-19. It was an online forum that became a source of support that superintendents could depend on for reliable information, as shown in figure 2.3.

According to the superintendents who started #suptchat, the goal of the networking opportunities was to help superintendents use social media to message in a positive way about their districts. Such messaging could allow superintendents to engage with their communities using technology they may have not been familiar with. The beauty of #suptchat was that it would pose a question in the chat, and then many superintendents would actively connect and engage virtually with their community. In a sense, superintendents gained an hour of professional development every time they joined #suptchat.

When superintendents faced a crisis such as COVID-19 that disrupted schooling, they were able to leverage informal networks like #suptchat. Superintendents were able to connect with others from districts that had experienced similar challenges, seek out solutions, and hear what was or was not working. The once-a-month opportunities also gave superintendents, regardless of whether they were already Twitter (now X) users or not, a model of how some districts use these platforms to communicate. Those who attended each session were shown the districts' stories and were also given the chance to have real-time learning experiences. The participants in #suptchat were learning how to increase their own digital learning capacity just by listening to "suptchat." It provided professional development, quick responses that served as immediate support, and practical strategies for emergency response and recovery.

INSIGHTS AND TAKEAWAYS FROM THE POWER OF NETWORKING

- *Shared experiences.* Networking gave superintendents the chance to share, compare, and learn from each other's successes and mistakes. This peer support was central in developing effective strategies for remote learning and crisis management. Superintendents who maintained strong networks found they had a support system to rely on for advice, moral support, and practical solutions during the pandemic.

- *Mentorship opportunities.* Experienced superintendents provided mentorship to their less-experienced counterparts, guiding them through the complexities of leading a district during a crisis. This mentorship often resulted in improved leadership capabilities and more resilient educational environments.
- *Access to diverse perspectives.* Engaging with a broader network exposes superintendents to diverse perspectives and innovative solutions. By tapping into the collective wisdom of their peers, they are able to implement more effective and creative approaches to problem-solving. This cross-pollination of ideas leads to the adoption of best practices from various districts, enhancing overall district performance.
- *Building resilient and viable systems.* Networking facilitated the identification of long-lasting practices that could be integrated into long-term strategies. The shared knowledge helped superintendents build more resilient systems capable of adapting to future challenges. Superintendents learned the importance of having robust contingency plans and the flexibility to pivot quickly in response to unforeseen events.
- *Resource sharing.* Virtual networks enabled the sharing of resources, such as lesson plans, technology tools, and professional development materials. This collaborative approach meant districts could avoid duplication of efforts and could ensure that all students had access to high-quality educational resources, regardless of their district's individual capacity.
- *Collaborative solutions.* Networking fostered a collaborative environment where superintendents could tackle complex problems together. This collective approach to problem-solving resulted in more comprehensive and well-rounded solutions. Superintendents learned that working together often yielded better results than working in isolation.

The COVID-19 pandemic served as a catalyst for significant changes in how superintendents manage school districts. Through informal and formal networking, superintendents shared their crisis management strategies and learned from the experiences of others. This exchange of knowledge helped them refine their own crisis-response plans and be better prepared for future emergencies. Those who embraced these lessons and used their networks for problem-solving emerged stronger and more resilient, demonstrating the value of collaboration and shared knowledge. As we move forward, these insights will help create more resilient and responsive educational environments.

NOTE

1. AASA, Early Learning Cohort, https://www.aasa.org/professional-learning/event/2024/08/14/default-calendar/early-learning-cohort.

Chapter 3

Relief Funding and Its Complex Legacy

The Effects of COVID-19 on School Budgets

> There was a tremendous amount of pressure to develop learning recovery programs that were stronger than what was in place pre-pandemic and at the same time a big push to spend the dollars quickly, so the public wouldn't question the necessity of the additional funding.
>
> —Dr. Kent P. Scribner, former superintendent, Fort Worth Independent School District, Texas

The Elementary and Secondary School Emergency Relief Fund (ESSER) was introduced in March of 2020 to help keep the economy and social systems going during lockdowns. It was part of the CARES Act (Coronavirus Aid Relief and Economic Security). It was the single largest federal investment in public education in the country's history.

Many K–12 school superintendents welcomed the much-needed federal relief funding program as they prepared to reopen schools safely, but they felt tremendous pressure to make plans quickly and spend the funds rapidly. Their districts were up against unrealistic timelines and harsh public criticism, both of which made prompt and decisive spending advisable.

As the virus was changing, the guidance given by state and federal agencies to school districts about how to best use the funds—while flexible and appreciated—contributed to the atmosphere of conflict. Parents and other stakeholders were often critical of how school districts were prioritizing and spending the ESSER funds. The public had ongoing criticism, for example, about factors such as when schools opened; if masks, social distancing, and contact tracing were required; and what, specifically, teachers were doing with the 20 percent requirement thought to be enough to mitigate the learning loss.

The different rounds of these federal funds had different purposes. ESSER funds primarily focused on three things at different times during the pandemic, but the main purpose of the funds was the safe reopening of schools. The focus of ESSER I was on triage and creating a safe reopening and return to in-person instruction. ESSER II focused on maintaining safe in-person learning, with support for schools to continue remote learning access and to incentivize learning during the summer break. ESSER II also supported the transition that students experienced as schools were reopening safely.

The American Rescue Plan (ARP ESSER) Act was signed into law on Thursday, March 11, 2021, and was distributed in the same manner as ESSER relief fund dollars. Primary fund use was to help schools "safely reopen and sustain" their operations and address the impact of COVID-19.[1]

ARP Funds, also known as ESSER III funds, in theory were to support innovative research to advance learning and the well-being of students and staff in school and remote settings. ESSER II and III were aimed more at enabling a safe return to learning in the classroom, encouraging initiatives to help make up for learning loss, and ensuring equity for historically disadvantaged groups.

ESSER funds were awarded to state education agencies (SEAs), and it was up to the SEAs to determine the proportions of allocations and to award funding to local education agencies within the state, such as school districts.

The broader implications of ESSER funding involve several issues. Many school districts were already underfunded before the pandemic. The ESSER funds, while substantial, were not sufficient to make up for years of budget cuts and underinvestment. Long-term problems such as deferred maintenance cannot be solved with short-term solutions like one-time funding. Effective, innovative ways to support learning and well-being take leadership and time for thoughtful planning.

THE SHORT- AND LONG-TERM AIMS OF ESSER:
"Adapting and adjusting according to feedback from stakeholders."

The push on the part of the government to inject funds into the economy quickly, to avoid another recession similar to the Great Recession of 2008, has sometimes seemed to be at odds with the original intention of the ESSER funds. Their original intention was to support students' safe return to schools and to support learning. While the need for quick spending of the funds necessitates a streamlined, expeditious process with a broad-stroke financial aim (to pump money into the economy), the ESSER funds ideally require a slower, longer-term process that involves reflection, consensus-building, and study. It is a process that can reasonably be expected to take a relatively long time, with its more people-focused aims relating to children's development, curriculum choices, educational approaches and philosophies, mental health needs, and the need to develop programs that work.

This problem of the funds seeming to have both short- and long-term aims may have contributed to some of the public's misperception of how schools and school districts managed the funds. The management of the funds often became a matter of contentious negotiation. Dr. David Schuler, former superintendent of Township High School District 214 in Illinois and current executive director of AASA, has considered these issues of how quickly the money was to be spent and how decisions were made about its allocation:

> Schools and school districts have done a remarkable job with managing the ESSER funds. Just because schools haven't spent their funds, doesn't mean the funds aren't encumbered. Schools and school districts did what they were expected to do, in terms of adapting and adjusting according to feedback from stakeholders. What I really appreciate about superintendents and school boards across the country is that over 40 percent of school districts indicated that they adapted their ESSER plans based on feedback from stakeholders. I am incredibly proud of that, and for the most part the criticism on the part of some isn't fair.

In other words, superintendents and school boards had a difficult task: to spend the money in accordance with ESSER guidelines and to plan and act quickly; to address students' pandemic-caused learning deficits, which takes time; to consider existing, long-standing educational needs that parents and others may prioritize; and to negotiate a balanced, favorable outcome.

Now in 2024, with the looming expiration of these federal funds, our schools face a substantial funding cliff, even though the challenges created by the pandemic largely remain. For the most part, public schools have done a commendable job rebounding from the pandemic. Recovery efforts have aided in addressing the learning deficits that many students experienced, with federal funds paying for extra help, like tutoring and summer school. But the loss of federal funding threatens to derail this progress, with many students still facing significant learning deficits caused by the pandemic.

Meanwhile, the gap between students from rich and poor communities, already huge before the pandemic, has widened. Continued investment is necessary to advance student academic achievement and to reduce racial and economic opportunity gaps. State leaders' obligation to ensure that all students have access to high-quality educational opportunities has not changed. In fact, this obligation is even more evident at this moment, as districts spend down the remaining funds. The access to millions of dollars allowing school districts to invest more deeply in meeting the social, emotional, and academic needs of their most marginalized students will end as ESSER funds expire on September 30, 2024.

SCHOOL BUDGETS BEFORE ESSER:
"We have always had to fight for funding."

Since the Great Recession of 2008, schools have had a difficult time recovering economically. Property taxes remain a primary source of funding for many schools, and in 2008, the amount of such real estate-related income plummeted due to the housing market crash. This decrease in property tax revenues has hurt schools, but so has other fiscal "belt-tightening." Governments at all levels faced shortfalls, which led to cuts in public services, including a reduction in per-student funding for education. As school budgets become more strained, the economic hardship placed on families increases, too, when the increased costs of support services and lunch prices get passed along to students.

The long-term consequences of the Great Recession are huge. Schools delayed necessary repairs and updates to facilities, often called deferred maintenance. Budget cuts resulted in teacher layoffs and larger class sizes, with reduced individualized attention for students. Extracurricular activities, art, special education programs, and physical education classes were often the first to be cut during this time. Some school districts haven't ever recovered to pre-recession funding levels.

The historical aspect of the Great Recession is important in helping to understand why schools remain underfunded and why the ESSER funds could not make up the difference. ESSER funds are non-recurring. They are intended for short-term relief and specific purposes, such as improving ventilation systems, providing personal protective equipment, and supporting remote learning infrastructure. They do not address long-term funding needs. Yet, many superintendents have concerns that states will believe that federal funds are enough to support schools, putting state funding formulas at risk.

The rules governing how ESSER funds can be used are complex and vary by state, making it difficult for the public to understand why certain needs are met while others are not. As noted above, some parents and community members had a misconception that the influx of ESSER funds would mean solving or improving many serious, long-standing financial issues with the schools.

In reality, these federal funds are marked for specific uses and do not cover ongoing operational costs. With the expiration of the funds coming due, schools and districts may struggle to effectively communicate how ESSER funds were utilized and what deficits still exist. Without clear, accessible information—regarding how the ESSER funds impacted learning loss, how they did or did not help recovery efforts, and what academic gaps remain—more skepticism and confusion could result regarding overall school district funding.

ESSER FUNDS:
"I was grateful for the funding, but mindful of the consequences."

ESSER funds were a lifeline for many schools during the pandemic, providing critical resources to maintain operations, ensure safety, and support remote learning. As these funds dwindle, schools face the challenge of sustaining the initiatives and improvements they enabled.

ESSER funds were appropriated in three federal laws. In March of 2020, Congress set aside approximately $13.2 billion of the $30.75 billion allotted to the Educational Stabilization Fund through the CARES Act for the ESSER Fund. The Coronavirus Response and Relief Supplemental Appropriations (CRRSA) Act, 2021, was signed into law on December 27, 2020, and provided an additional $54.3 billion for the ESSER II Fund. ESSER II Fund awards were allocated to state agencies in the same proportion as each state receives Part A of Title 1 of the Elementary and Secondary Education Act of 1965, as amended, in fiscal year 2020.

In March 2021, superintendents learned the last round of funding, $1.9 trillion, included $122 billion for ARP ESSER Fund dollars and would be distributed in the same manner as the previous ESSER funds.[2]

Here is a breakdown of the primary uses of ESSER funds:

- *Technology and infrastructure*: Schools invested heavily in technology to facilitate remote learning. This investment included purchasing laptops, tablets, and internet hotspots for students, as well as upgrading infrastructure to support online education.
- *Health and safety measures*: Funds were used to implement health protocols, such as purchasing personal protective equipment (PPE), enhancing cleaning regimens, and improving ventilation systems to reduce the spread of COVID-19.
- *Academic support*: To mitigate learning loss, many schools hired additional staff, extended learning time through summer schools or after-school programs, and invested in tutoring services.
- *Mental health services*: Recognizing the pandemic's toll on students' mental health, schools allocated funds for counseling services, social-emotional learning (SEL) programs, and training for staff to better support students.

- *Professional development*: Teachers and staff received training to adapt to new teaching methods and technologies, ensuring they could effectively deliver instruction in a remote or hybrid model.

The grant funds were disbursed to state departments of education with a legislative mandate to pass 90 percent of the money directly to school districts to help them safely reopen schools, continue operating during the COVID-19 pandemic, and address the many harmful effects of the pandemic on students. Later that first year, though, it became clear that schools and districts would need to address the pandemic's broader impacts on students. Many of the superintendents interviewed for this book recalled that their earliest expenditures were on establishing safe learning environments. These investments included shifting to remote learning; investing in masks, sanitizing, and COVID testing; creating classrooms in expanded areas or outdoors to facilitate social distancing; and seeking to clean indoor air.

Superintendents' later efforts focused more on learning acceleration, especially through tutoring, summer learning, curriculum changes, and on addressing the mental and behavioral health impacts on students of social isolation and grief. Federal rules reflected these shifting priorities. As noted above, it was only with ESSER III, signed into law in March 2021, that Congress introduced a requirement for a large portion of the money, 20 percent, to be spent on addressing learning loss.

Many schools experienced significant enrollment decline after COVID-19. The most recently available federal data indicates that public K–12 enrollment declined by about 1.4 million students from 2019 to 2021, or about 2.2 percent, an immense percentage drop. The lower enrollments are due to several factors, including a decades-long birth rate decline across the country; increase in homeschooling; a move to private schools and other school options; the expansion of voucher programs; and more children not being registered for school and thus not being accounted for. When districts enroll fewer students, they generate less revenue through their state's funding formula. It was hoped and expected that student numbers would bounce back as the pandemic curved, but the rebound has not yet come to pass.

Schools and students were experiencing a lot of uncertainty, so to reduce stress, some districts made decisions early on to do as much as they could to reduce the impact of enrollment declines on school budgets. Dr. Scott A. Menzel, superintendent of Scottsdale Unified School District, said, "We provided money to hold schools harmless for enrollment declines and avoided making large cuts. Helping schools to stabilize their enrollments with ESSER funds was huge."

CHALLENGES WITH ESSER:
"It was a lot of money all at once, yet tricky timelines for spending."

ESSER funding helped students in every district and from every background recover from pandemic-induced declines in test scores. However, not all districts received the same funding per student. The federal government wisely targeted funding to the low-income communities that tended to suffer disproportionate harm from the pandemic. Funds were distributed through the same formula as federal Title I education funding, which allocates more resources to districts with a high proportion of low-income families than to wealthier districts.

It is important to highlight the fund distribution amounts per state because schools that received more dollars per the allocation are at risk for losing more as the ESSER funds end. In terms of recovery efforts, the students most at risk are those in poor districts, whose test scores fell further during the pandemic. Those are the students who need much more than their peers from higher-income families to catch up and who may never catch up. Students in poor communities are at a greater disadvantage today than they were five years ago with more needs. And meeting those needs costs more, too. As the ESSER funds end, many students will still need significant support. As figure 3.1 shows, the U.S. Department of Education provides a resource for the public to view how COVID-19 recovery and relief funds have been allocated and spent by state.

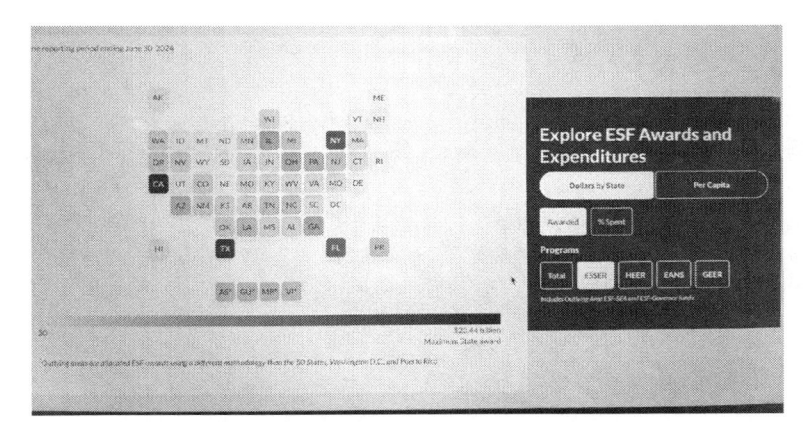

Figure 3.1. State distribution amounts during funding periods showing ESSER awards and expenditure dollars by state and per capita. *Source*: U.S. Department of Education. Institute of Education Sciences, National Center for Education Statistics. covid-relief-data.

ESSER funding helped improve the overall equity of school funding in many states as a one-time funding allocation. That is, ESSER funding was generally distributed in accordance with student needs. This policy on distribution helped to offset opportunity gaps that widened dramatically during the pandemic for students from working-class families with low incomes and for students of color.

With the expiration of ESSER funding, some state school funding will likely become less equitable and less adequate. Changes to the formulas that allocate federal Title 1 funds require a reauthorization of ESEA, which is required to occur every five years but doesn't always occur on that timeline with Congress. Unless state leaders step up to replace expiring funding or otherwise move to improve the adequacy and equity of the state's school funding, then students—particularly those from historically marginalized communities—will pay the biggest price.

WIDENED INEQUALITY *WITHIN* DISTRICTS:
"We need more time to impact student learning."

As recovery efforts proceeded, it became clear that children from wealthier districts benefited from resources faster. Researchers have analyzed data available in fifteen states and schools within districts. They found that districts that spend resources like ESSER funds on services like tutoring and transportation for tutoring, *coupled with families who can access those services*, are more likely to benefit than districts with low-earning parents who cannot access services or possibly attract more experienced teachers.[3]

Even when schools offered interventions to help students catch up, lower-income families might have been less able to rearrange schedules or transportation to ensure their children attended. The data indicate that Black students, on average, are now recovering at a faster pace than white or Hispanic students, but because they lost more ground than white students, they remain further behind. In the context of the expiration of ESSER funds, we must move forward to close the achievement gaps between students. Superintendents will need to identify programs that successfully worked to close the student achievement gaps.

Superintendents felt that the timelines for spending the funds were neither appropriate nor sufficient for such a large grant. For large Title 1 districts, it can be difficult to spend hundreds of millions of dollars on one-time expenditures within the short timelines required for ESSER funds. Dr. Baron Davis, former superintendent of Richland School District Two in South Carolina, commented on the issue of timelines:

My chief takeaways from the ESSER period were that spending timelines should match the size of the allocation. Spending well and responsibly in the time frame provided, he said, "probably made this already chaotic period of COVID-19 and post-COVID-19 a lot more challenging than it needed to be, and just a lot of chaos in terms of how to spend dollars well in the best interest of students."

Deadlines are a particular issue in the context of efforts to address learning loss. As recent testing data and research indicate, the impact of disrupted schooling on students' academic growth is ongoing and seems likely to outlast the final ESSER spending deadline.[4] Additional funding will be required to address learning gaps. Many superintendents believed strongly that if the deadlines had been extended, strategies to target learning loss might have been more effective.

In most cases, when districts received their ESSER allocations, they started out with a plan: to adhere to the directive to spend dollars by the deadline to keep students safe while learning. Next, district leaders would attempt to address long-standing needs that were also connected to pandemic problems. It was hard, however, as Scribner said, to sort out what was an "immediate and emergent need" rather than a long-deferred investment. For instance, 20 percent of ESSER III funds had to be spent on evidence-based efforts to accelerate learning, but academic opportunity and learning gaps had long preceded the pandemic. He explained, "You have an infusion of money right now to spend. You *must* earmark a certain percentage of it for learning loss." Air filters and outdoor classrooms were clearly new needs, even though aging air conditioning or heating systems and poor air quality were long-standing problems in many older school buildings.

Initiatives like improving district literacy instruction and training educators in SEL strategies, though, were meant to address issues that both existed before the pandemic and were worsened by it. Districts benefited greatly from the investment of the ESSER funds when their priority was identifying programs that worked to improve learning efficiently, systems that report on outcomes in an accurate and timely manner, and ways to communicate to community members about programs that positively impacted students.

When it came to spending a large amount within the allotted time, districts often found that the advice to avoid using the money for recurring costs, like staff salaries, was hard to apply in practice. Eighty percent of the school district's annual budget is salaries and benefits, and then probably a good majority of the rest of the outgoing costs go to outside contractors, basically providing services and labor. From a financial management perspective, the size of the distribution was a main reason that many districts felt they had to use the money to hire and pay employees. Education is indeed a "people business." Practically all worthwhile initiatives require instructional or support staff. While smaller amounts were spent on goods like personal protective equipment, technology, and curricular materials, it likely would have triggered accusations of wasteful spending to use all the relief money for things that could be bought without any hiring. Other districts, when they could find staff to hire, settled on an approach that combined uses of funds to hire tutors and to purchase curriculum to support academic and health and wellness needs that best supported students.

POSITIVE IMPACT OF ESSER FUNDING:
"The funds allowed us to do things we wouldn't have otherwise been able to do."

In Arizona, Scottsdale Unified School District Superintendent Dr. Scott Menzel affirmed that because ESSER funds functioned as extra money and decisions about them couldn't imperil core staff or services, "we could really dig in on strategy." One example was his district's ESSER-supported shift to support a supplemental English language arts curriculum. New curricula are expensive and require a significant investment in staff training to implement well. With the support of ESSER dollars, the district was able to purchase and fully implement a high-quality, research-backed supplemental curriculum. He described their process:

> We were able to provide supplemental curriculum that focused on personalized and targeted support for students. We could support our educators with a strong implementation plan that helps accelerate student learning. That was really important because we were also able to support teachers by purchasing supplemental curriculum that helped support students and saved them time it would normally take for them to design and plan for instruction.

For Menzel, these dollars provided not just curricular materials but also much-needed support for his teachers and staff.

As in many states across the country, Arizona schools are not funded at a level commensurate with need. The additional supplemental curriculum "was an effective use of funds," said Menzel, and one "that would have been really nearly impossible, because of funding models, to do on their own in such a robust way." In addition to being able to support teachers with additional materials, Menzel saw other benefits:

> We tried to use this as an opportunity to let go. I think it's so hard in a state where you are underfunded, where you often feel like you're operating from

a mindset of scarcity, it's really hard to let anything go. With extra dollars, it was possible to have more critical conversations about current services, programs, and staff roles, and schools became more willing to jettison ineffective approaches.

Schools and districts could also set aside funding to assess the impact of new initiatives. Some districts are budgeting for the evaluation of several ESSER-backed programs, with the goal that evidence of success will inspire state and local lawmakers to sustain those efforts after ESSER dollars are gone.

ESSER III funds allowed superintendents to pursue innovative changes. This part of the funding program dovetailed well with superintendents' existing work—evaluating the effectiveness of core instructional programs and looking for new ways to pursue better student outcomes. ESSER III, in effect, encouraged such pursuit of innovation. State funding formulas are key to sustaining the innovation. Not everything schools try will work, but having dollars to try things differently is key to helping teachers and students exist in the "new normal" that is being defined post-COVID-19. ESSER funds gave schools the chance to try different technology platforms, maintain innovative hardware and software, sustain wellness programs for students, and expand high-dose tutoring curriculum and staffing. High-dose tutoring includes at least three interactions per week with students, lasting at least thirty minutes, with a student-to-tutor ratio of three to one.

The ESSER funds were also a great source to help educators identify priorities, pay for enrichment activities to enhance the curriculum (for students who need above-and-beyond learning), and pay for teachers to collectively meet and analyze grade-level standards.

Dr. Martha Salazar-Zamora, superintendent of Tomball Independent School District in Texas, oversaw a district that saw not only improvement in student academics but also growth in enrollment during the pandemic. She found that the ESSER funds brought new energy and attention:

> We were pushed to do things we have always known we were capable of. Parents were attentive to the work of our teachers, assessments online, paying particular attention to how often students were paying attention to tasks teachers were asking of them.

The district used COVID-19 dollars to put in place specialized teachers trained to support students but was clear from the beginning that once the funding was gone, regardless of impact and even if the needs continued, the positions would end. Salazar-Zamora credits the work of teachers and caregivers with establishing the district's overall A+ rating.

Collaboration among levels of government had a positive effect in creating opportunities for better student outcomes. The fact that cities and towns also received federal relief dollars meant that many school districts were in counties or towns that received their own sizable relief allocations, necessitating a collaborative effort on the part of all stakeholders. The realities revealed by the pandemic made clear the need for collaboration and a focus on community issues beyond academics. Menzel said:

> Even now, I think a lot of folks are just focused on academic proficiency and proficiency rates. I think we all want students to graduate, improve academically, and grow, but I think what we've learned through the pandemic is that schools serve a broader need for children, for a family, and for the community at large.

Menzel, as others have, saw addressing the "broader need," beyond academics, as important. One of the clearest examples was feeding students and families through expanded school nutrition programs. Unfortunately, these programs have now ended in many states. Menzel also saw it in the challenge of sustaining funding to meet needs not traditionally thought of as educational concerns but that were revealed as school functions when schools were impacted by building closures and the transition to remote learning. These needs are community-wide, as Menzel said:

> Any time we can look at them from a collective impact framework, I think it helps all of us align goals, even strengthen policymaking because the same community-based organization—school, employer, faith-based organizations, and groups—we all serve the same community. I think we were forced to collaborate and work together, and we formed some amazing partnerships. The community maximized our collective efforts to support the children and families that we all serve.

While successes like those Menzel described were certainly not universal, they do support the idea that there may be value in funding different but geographically overlapping units of government at the same time, promoting collaboration between school districts, towns, counties, and other entities that have distinct capabilities but are responsible for the same communities.

MITIGATING THE FUNDING CLIFF:
"We had to remember these were one-time dollars."

The negative impacts of these funding cliffs fall hardest on Black families and working-class families with low incomes. State lawmakers must act to replace these expiring federal funding streams with state funding. Failure to do so will derail pandemic recovery and exacerbate racial and economic opportunity gaps that hamstring many states' ability to create a multiracial democracy and an economy where all can flourish.

Already, many districts have made tough choices, such as staff layoffs, program reductions, and program eliminations. In some instances, districts are contemplating school closures to balance their budgets. Districts are grappling with ESSER funds expiring and the continued loss of buying power as increased labor costs and other costs, such as technology and energy, make it more expensive for many districts to operate. In places with declining school enrollment, state actions aimed at addressing revenue shortfalls are most harmful for districts serving the most students of color and students from low-income backgrounds.

When states cut budgets to balance their budgets amid sharp revenue declines during the Great Recession of 2008, high-poverty districts that were more reliant on state aid suffered the most. If state economies enter a recession, districts serving the most students of color and students from low-income backgrounds will be further vulnerable to budget shortfalls. State and district leaders can and should budget equitably beyond ESSER. With inequities in student experiences and learning outcomes now exacerbated, advocates must double down on their efforts to hold state and district leaders accountable for equitably investing in students of color and students from low-income backgrounds.

The primary takeaway from ESSER funds is this: Schools still have tremendous work to do in the wake of COVID-19, especially addressing learning losses and mental health issues facing students and staff. There is no denying the ESSER funds provided necessary relief for pandemic-related issues. Funds are still necessary, however, to mitigate needs. The funds allowed schools to safely reopen and return students to in-person learning. The timelines for spending and reporting expenditure periods should have been extended past 2025 to allow for thoughtful auditing and planning for appropriate and best usage of each usage period. State legislatures would have been less likely to view federal funds as inappropriate and therefore usurp their authority to increase the state funding formulas for historically underfunded public schools. When additional federal funds come into play with annual or biannual state legislature budgets, the priority to restore recession cuts to public education is unfortunately often forgotten.

With the end of ESSER funding comes increased pressure on district finance teams to plan for sustainability. The ending of this large federal revenue stream presents an opportunity to evaluate what is currently funded and to establish priority goals to permanently build in the resource allocations. It also gives superintendents an opportunity to communicate with stakeholders at the state and national levels about the need for ongoing investments in K–12 education and to advocate for funding based on what impacts student academics, health, and wellness initiatives.

Districts should use data to help state leaders see evidence-based practices that help students maintain or increase learning levels. Further, the data is also key in helping stakeholders see how districts managed and maximized the use of ESSER funds during all rounds of the funding windows.

EXEMPLARY LEADERSHIP: DR. DEB KERR, SUPERINTENDENT OF ST. FRANCIS PUBLIC SCHOOL DISTRICT, WISCONSIN

Some superintendents, especially those who serve in smaller districts and who received smaller allocations, felt they did not have enough time to make good use of the funds. Dr. Deborah Kerr is superintendent of St. Francis Public School District in Wisconsin, which enrolls just under 2,000 students and received a total of $2 million in ESSER funds. She explained that in the early part of the pandemic, the district dealt with safety and technology expenses, as well as increases in staff costs, when new employees were needed to cover for other people's paid medical leaves. While it was beneficial to have dollars that came quickly but did not come with immediate spending mandates, later funds with tight timelines have not proven to be as helpful, as Kerr noted:

> As ESSER II and III funds came we needed more flexibility to deal with the increased challenges in mental health needs we saw with both students and staff. What would have helped more was greater flexibility in the timelines, in terms of incorporating the money into budget cycles from year to year. We are still seeing in our early grades the gaps in learning that we didn't expect, so having extended time to make the best use of those funds to help students recoup for learning loss would have been helpful.

Kerr explained that having even one additional year to invest in ESSER II funds would have helped her to plan for what she now knows are her students' needs. Her district generally operates on a lean budget, without a large staff. Kerr knew that using most of the funds to support staff and students who were suffering emotionally would be the best way to help them recover from the pandemic. She recalls relying on the theory of Maslow's hierarchy of needs to assist staff and students first before addressing students' academic needs.

Kerr said that while she was serving as superintendent for the Brown Deer School District in Wisconsin, she focused on the health and wellness of students over education-specific needs. In this district, the community understood the importance of focusing first on health and wellness before anything else:

> We didn't focus on academics first because we didn't have to. We had to focus on making sure our kids had food. Being in a district with 60 percent poverty and 80 percent minority students, our first task was to be sure our kids were taken care of. Food stations set up across the street from the elementary school that contained supplies like diapers and Kleenex were helpful.

Kerr recalled the community church being visited by families, often for food and supplies, and by one of her families who just had their house burned down. "This mother with three kids had absolutely no access to anything." The types of students' school-related needs changed over time, including them having to deal with the effects of having long been at home, out of the classroom," Kerr continued:

> I am proud that our community was able to come together and provide resources for the mother whose home was destroyed by the fire during this time. While we were focused on the mental health and well-being of the kids and families, we really didn't know what the impact would be like long term. When we returned to in-person learning, we focused on getting students what they needed most, and that was more for mental health services.

Like many other superintendents, those who partnered with families—and community organizations like churches—were able to fulfill the basic needs of students and families in their communities. They could help, even when emergencies happened during and after the pandemic, in ways they otherwise would not have been able to.

Kerr's account highlights the important point that students and families did not experience the pandemic in the same way at the same time. In responding to the pandemic, each district had to consider local circumstances and challenging issues that were being faced. These considerations often meant using the funds to address long-standing needs or, in districts without high pre-pandemic staff-to-student ratios, increasing staff to address new problems or address emergency situations.

Moving forward, evaluating the impact of ESSER funds will involve establishing clear metrics and methodologies to assess the funds' effectiveness in improving educational outcomes. Key areas of measurement include:

- Monitoring student performance—through standardized test scores, grades, and other assessments designed to gauge improvements in academic achievement and learning recovery—and sharing those results in a transparent way with all stakeholders;

- Tracking student attendance and engagement in both in-person and remote learning environments to identify trends and address barriers to participation; and
- Measuring improvements in student well-being, assessing the availability and use of mental health services, conducting surveys, and gathering feedback from students, parents, and staff.

This was a historic investment in our public education system that superintendents had the responsibility to allocate strategically, under incredibly trying circumstances, and with very little time. They did so with a focus on strengthening their school systems so that every staff member and student received the support they needed.

INSIGHTS AND TAKEAWAYS FROM THE EFFECTS OF COVID-19 ON SCHOOL BUDGETS

- Maintain transparency in planning, implementation, and reporting to build trust and accountability among stakeholders. This approach includes regular updates and accessible reporting mechanisms.
- Develop long-term plans that integrate ESSER-funded initiatives into sustainable programs, ensuring continued support and impact beyond the funding period. Allow for flexibility in fund utilization to adapt to changing needs and circumstances while maintaining adherence to overarching goals and guidelines.
- Foster collaboration between federal, state, and local authorities, as well as with community organizations to leverage resources and expertise.
- Implement robust monitoring and evaluation frameworks to continuously assess the impact of interventions and make data-driven adjustments as needed. While collecting accurate and comprehensive data to assess needs, track spending, and measure outcomes can be challenging, particularly for smaller districts with limited capacity, it is critical for planning. It also is vital in maintaining trust within the community.
- Annually engage stakeholders in budgeting to ensure that plans align with student needs. Assess programmatic areas and adjust resources to match student needs so students are no longer disproportionately impacted by the pandemic.
- Communicate the priorities of the strategic budget to schools, community members, and state leaders. Include a way to engage with them so they understand how to better help implement school and district goals.

Achieving consensus among diverse stakeholders with differing priorities and perspectives can be difficult, yet it is essential for superintendents and school leaders to ensure the effective implementation of key initiatives.

NOTES

1. Elementary and Secondary School Emergency Relief Fund, Department of Education, Office of Elementary and Secondary Education, https://oese.ed.gov/offices/education-stabilization-fund/elementary-secondary-school-emergency-relief-fund/.

2. Elementary and Secondary School Emergency Relief Fund, Department of Education, Office of Elementary and Secondary Education, https://oese.ed.gov/offices/education-stabilization-fund/elementary-secondary-school-emergency-relief-fund/.

3. Carrie Spector, "New Report Shows Historic Gains in Pandemic Recovery for many U.S. School Districts," *Research Stories*, Stanford Graduate School of Education, January 31, 2024, https://ed.stanford.edu/news/new-report-shows-historic-gains-pandemic-recovery-many-us-school-districts.

4. Erin M. Fahle et al., "School District and Community Factors Associated with Learning Loss During the COVID-19 Pandemic," Center for Education Policy Research at Harvard University and Educational Opportunity Project at Stanford University (May 2023): 1–65, https://cepr.harvard.edu/sites/hwpi.harvard.edu/files/cepr/files/explaining_covid_losses_5.23.pdf.

Chapter 4

Creating a Culture of Care for Students and Staff

> We built a virtual and hybrid learning system on the fly, with no prior experience or roadmap.
>
> —Dr. Aaron Spence, Superintendent, Loudoun County Public Schools, Virginia

While the duration of school closures varied from state to state, in the early days of the pandemic, all public schools in the nation shut their doors, sending students and staff home with little preparation or time to adjust. Ensuring that students could access learning from home, however, was only part of the challenge. For many superintendents, their priority was seeing that their students' basic needs were met by providing daily meals and physical and mental health support. The fact that meeting basic needs looked vastly different in districts across the country only underscored the inequities that were, and are, endemic to our education system. All of us, particularly those serving significant populations of students living in poverty, needed to provide meals and, in some cases, telehealth, as well as devices and internet access. The idea of educating the "whole child" truly took on new meaning in 2020.

Beyond helping address students' basic needs, superintendents needed to do all they could—and quickly—to make sure students continued with their education under the challenging circumstances of the COVID-19 pandemic. Superintendents were instrumental in leading these efforts to provide students with devices, internet access, software, and high-quality instruction. The scale of this challenge for districts was largely dependent on how significant their digital divide was pre-COVID-19. For example, for those districts that were already "1:1," meaning they had a device assigned to every student, device distribution was not as much of a challenge. For others, however, purchasing new devices and making sure that every student needing one received one as quickly as possible consumed virtually all their time in the early weeks of the pandemic.

The shift to remote learning required a massive mobilization on the part of schools to meet the needs of students, staff, and families while school buildings were closed. Providing academic continuity compelled superintendents and their teams to simultaneously create plans for remote learning, hybrid learning, and ultimately a return to in-person learning.

SHIFTING TO REMOTE LEARNING:
"We were relentless in ensuring that kids stayed connected to us."

The digital divide had never been more front and center than it was during the pandemic, and an immediate challenge was making sure that every student had a working device at home.

For most superintendents, this was not a challenge school districts could address alone. Dr. Kyla Johnson-Trammell, superintendent in the Oakland Unified School District in California, contacted her city's mayor and, in doing so, helped launch a community-wide movement in support of her students.

I reached out to our mayor, who was able to get a pretty big donation of $10 million from Twitter. We just went public with that and just did joint fundraising. Of course, once you get one big donor like that, others start jumping on, so that we could do a massive purchase for computers. And so, that's what kind of started the whole "Oakland Undivided" campaign that became a national success. We worked with community-based organizations. Working together, we were able to ensure that all of our students who historically didn't have a device got one.

Johnson-Trammell knew that the scale of the challenge ahead of her meant she could not go it alone, so like many of her colleagues across the country, she leveraged the relationships she had built within her community to ensure that all students had what they need.

Providing devices to every student, however, did not guarantee that students could attend their classes remotely—a device not connected to the internet was little more than a glorified paperweight. Superintendents knew that the need was particularly acute for their students living in poverty and that the pandemic had further exacerbated the digital divide. Researchers confirmed that "what was a gap is now a chasm," when referring to widening gaps between those students who were equipped to attend school remotely and those who were not.[1] In fact, "one study highlighted that only two-thirds of youth in U.S. households with incomes less than $25,000 had computer and internet access for their children to engage in remote schooling."[2] To address this pervasive challenge, superintendents had to be creative problem-solvers.

Dr. Scott Muri formed an innovative partnership with SpaceX so that "every family needing home internet got home internet." Others, like Dr. Gregory Hutchings, Jr. in Alexandria City Public Schools, looked to local cable providers for help:

> We worked out an agreement with our cable company to provide free broadband for all of our families who did not have it. We had to go through their system and their customer service team, which was a challenge for some of our non-English-speaking families. We also set up a help desk. There were so many logistics, but I would say that within the first month all of our students not only had computers but also internet.

In some cases, simply acquiring an adequate number of hot spots to distribute was all superintendents could do, and that was not easy. The rapid transition to remote learning also required the rapid deployment of online learning platforms and tools, coordinating with IT departments to get teachers and students access to the necessary technology. This deployment involved not only selecting and implementing appropriate digital platforms like Google Classroom, Microsoft Teams, or Zoom but also training students and their families to use them effectively.

PROVIDING MEALS:
"We were literally feeding the town."

In 2022, over 30 million students received a free or reduced-priced lunch through the National School Lunch Program. This number represents over 60 percent of all public school students.[3] When schools closed during the pandemic, many students who had relied on school for not only lunch but sometimes breakfast as well were at risk of going hungry. Fortunately, the U.S. Department of Agriculture, which administers the National School Lunch Program, relaxed its rules during the pandemic and allowed districts to distribute meals to anyone under 18.[4] They also allowed parents or family members to pick up meals for their children since they were not receiving them directly at school. Superintendents, along with district and school staff, had to organize meal distribution efforts so that students, and, in many cases, their families, were fed, as illustrated in figure 4.1. They set up grab-and-go meal sites at schools and other community locations, delivered meals to students' homes, and coordinated with local food banks and organizations to supplement these efforts. Every superintendent interviewed developed some

Figure 4.1. Staff in Highline Public Schools preparing to distribute meals to students and families. *Source*: Photograph courtesy of Tove Tupper.

kind of daily or weekly meal distribution plan for students and families, which they continued for months.

Managing the logistics of distributing meals, however, was not nearly as difficult as managing the emotions of it. One superintendent we interviewed recalled handing out meals at a drive-through distribution location one day and having a mother tell her that what she was receiving was the only food in their house for the week. As Dr. Candy Singh, former superintendent for Fallbrook Union Elementary School District in California, said, "We really were feeding everybody in our community."

SUPPORTING STUDENTS' EMOTIONAL WELL-BEING:
"Students first. Always."

The pandemic significantly impacted students' mental health,[5] and superintendents recognized the need to create robust support systems. Enfield still vividly remembers one interaction with a grandmother while distributing meals in the district parking lot in the early weeks of the pandemic:

I would always ask families how things were at home, and on this day a woman just began crying so I asked her to pull over so we could talk. When I asked what was wrong, she explained that her teenage grandson with special needs had regressed so much from being out of school that all he did was silently walk around their kitchen in circles. She begged me through tears to bring him back into school. At that moment we were under state orders to remain closed so there was nothing I could do. As a leader I felt completely helpless. I knew our students and families were suffering, and I couldn't do anything for them. It was gut-wrenching.

Superintendents across the country had similar realizations and implemented district-wide mental health initiatives, which included virtual counseling services, wellness check-ins, and social-emotional learning (SEL) programs. Superintendents allocated resources to hire additional counselors and trained existing staff to recognize and respond to signs of distress in students.

MAINTAINING CONNECTION:
"We were relentless in ensuring that kids stayed connected to us."

While providing all students with home internet so they could log on to their classes was important, connection took on a much deeper meaning while schools were closed. Superintendents and their staff knew they had to make sure that students stayed connected to their friends and teachers. To counteract the isolation that many were experiencing during remote learning, superintendents encouraged schools to maintain social connections through virtual extracurricular activities. They supported the creation of online clubs, virtual sports practices, and other interactive events. These activities helped students stay connected to their peers and provided a sense of normalcy and community during a tumultuous time. In some districts, teachers coordinated drive-by parades in their students' neighborhoods with signs telling them how much they loved and missed them, as illustrated in figure 4.2.

Perhaps the greatest example of the lengths to which educators went to keep students connected to their schools, classmates, and teachers came during commencement season in 2020. States were still prohibiting large, in-person gatherings, making traditional commencement ceremonies out of the question, so districts adapted and got creative. Superintendents and their teams arranged for drive-through ceremonies, giving students their celebratory moment without violating state orders prohibiting large, in-person gatherings as illustrated in figures 4.3 and 4.4. While far from the traditional ceremony that students, staff, and families had looked forward to, it was a very public demonstration of the

Figure 4.2. Students in Highline Public Schools watching their teachers drive by their home to wave hello while schools were closed. *Source*: Photograph courtesy of Angela Burgess.

love and dedication educators had for their students. Many graduates admitted it was an event they would always remember.

CARING FOR STAFF:
"They needed to know how much we cared."

While supporting students was the priority for superintendents, they also knew they had to provide commensurate support to their staff—many of whom were also struggling. Similar to students, meeting the basic needs of staff was top of mind. This support started with making sure that staff were not suffering from the isolation of being home. Singh took deliberate steps with her team to address this potential for isolation:

> We knew we had to create systems of support, so we asked every school and department to identify a Care Team. These were teams of eight to ten people who took the lead in making sure that we didn't have a single person sitting home alone, not connected. I was especially worried about our older workers, and particularly our support staff, for whom being separate from their "work family" could have been devastating.

Focusing on her staff's emotional well-being was Singh's first priority, but quickly she and other superintendents around the country realized that they

Figure 4.3. Superintendent Susan Enfield congratulating a member of the Raisbeck Aviation High School in Washington state Class of 2020, during drive-through ceremony.
Source: Photograph courtesy of Susan Enfield.

also had to find ways to keep their staff members employed in a remote work environment.

When schools closed, there were certificated staff members, such as teachers, principals, counselors, and many in central office, whose work remained the same. For classified or support staff, however, such as bus drivers who were no longer transporting students on a daily basis and others such as custodians and paraprofessionals, districts had to be creative and partner with their unions and state officials to find alternative roles for them. The "what"

Figure 4.4. **Highline High School teachers and staff cheering for Class of 2020 graduates during their drive-through ceremony.** *Source*: Photo courtesy of Tove Tupper.

here was just as important as the "how," as highlighted by Dr. Joe Gothard, superintendent in the Madison Metropolitan School District in Wisconsin and former superintendent in St. Paul Public Schools in Minnesota. He emphasized the need for "great empathy" during this process and recalled the risk he took to keep his staff employed:

> We made sure that we weren't creating upheaval for people . . . I remember telling Human Resources to not adjust any staffing [since] I had no idea what the Fall was going to look like, and I didn't want to put people out of work. That was kind of a leap of faith, but I felt like it was the right decision to make. I had to take care of my people.

A big part of this process was also acknowledging people's emotions, especially the fear and sense of uncertainty that so many were experiencing. In Fallbrook, Singh and her team "acknowledged people's emotional state and fear by doubling the pay of support staff to acknowledge them as first responders." They also found new roles for support staff, such as paying them to help with childcare at local community organizations. As the interviews in this book have made clear, empathy was critical during this time, and in many ways, superintendents became a new kind of CEO—the Chief Empathy Officer.

DEPLOYING DEVICES AND PROFESSIONAL DEVELOPMENT:
"We had to help teachers and staff become tech-savvy quickly."

To maintain educational continuity during the pandemic, teachers needed to be able to effectively deliver online instruction, and the learning curve was greater for some than others. Educators' proficiency with technology was a critical component of education during COVID-19. Superintendents had to facilitate the adoption of user-friendly digital platforms and tools for virtual instruction. This commitment included investing in learning management systems (LMS) such as Canvas to organize assignments and other systems like Google Classroom, Microsoft Teams, and Zoom to hold classes. While these systems were in use in districts pre-pandemic, having to rely on them so heavily required a massive training effort. District staff provided virtual professional development, but teachers also stepped up to help one another. Those who were more proficient shared their knowledge and expertise with their peers, creating virtual professional learning communities.

Even with training and tools in place and the sharing of expertise, virtual learning proved challenging. Districts had to work with their teachers, and in many states with their teachers' unions, to determine the amount of synchronous versus asynchronous instruction the teachers would provide each day. Hutchings and his team deliberately limited instructional time because they quickly realized that trying to do a full eight-hour school day via Zoom simply did not work. It was too difficult for teachers to keep an entire class of students engaged for extended periods of time. In response, Hutchings's district created office hours where teachers could connect with students one-on-one, in addition to whole-group instruction. Singh and her team shifted their instructional model, prioritizing student engagement by encouraging learners to explore their passions, interests, and future careers through meaningful projects rather than traditional worksheets.

In addition, staff and students had to deal with whatever was happening in their homes during the school day, which often meant they were distracted or even incapable of engaging in schoolwork, for whatever reason. Learning from home meant balancing family responsibilities with class time and schoolwork, sometimes simultaneously. For teachers and staff, seeing their students from home via Zoom gave them a first-ever look into the lives of their students outside of school, and for some, what they saw was a startling reality. Superintendents and principals had to help teachers manage the emotions of this experience, which meant ensuring they had enough support systems available to staff who needed them.

MAINTAINING STAFF MORALE:
"We had to keep people going."

There is no question that the pandemic took a significant toll on the emotional and mental well-being of educators. Superintendents recognized the importance of supporting their staff in this area and implemented strategies to address these needs. Superintendents increased access to mental health resources, such as counseling services and Employee Assistance Programs. They facilitated partnerships with mental health organizations to offer virtual counseling sessions, workshops on stress management, and resources for self-care. These efforts not only provided staff with the tools to cope with the anxiety and stress caused by the pandemic but also signaled that their district leaders were investing in their mental health. In the words of Hutchings, "it showed that we cared about their humanity."

Superintendents initiated programs to promote emotional well-being, such as peer support groups and wellness initiatives. These programs encouraged staff to connect with one another, share their experiences, and offer support. Superintendents like Dr. LaTonya Goffney, in Aldine Independent School District near Houston, Texas, recognized that she and her team needed to show that they were listening to staff and meeting their needs as best they could:

> We hosted zooms where our district SEL [Social-Emotional Learning] team would go over breathing exercises to help people manage stress and anxiety. We also held virtual yoga sessions. You name it, we did it, including giving teachers the gift of time by canceling meetings and encouraging them to just take time for what they needed.

They also launched a social media campaign called #AldineCares to share all the ways the district staff were going above and beyond for their students and families, while also encouraging one another as colleagues. In many ways, this was nothing new since superintendents have always cared for their staff. During the pandemic, however, they had to demonstrate that care in more tangible ways to help staff manage their stress and stay healthy.

Recognizing the hard work and dedication of staff was essential in maintaining morale. Superintendents implemented programs to acknowledge and celebrate the efforts of teachers and support staff. Virtual award ceremonies, shout-outs in newsletters, and personalized messages of appreciation were some ways superintendents showed gratitude for their staff's commitment. Acknowledging the challenges and celebrating successes were instrumental in creating positive and motivating work environments at a time when people needed it the most.

EXEMPLARY LEADERSHIP: DR. THERESA ROUSE ON CARING FOR STUDENTS

Dr. Theresa Rouse became superintendent of Joliet Public Schools District 86 in 2016. The district, located in Joliet, Illinois, spans 26.4 square miles and serves nearly 10,000 K–8 students in 15 elementary schools, four junior high schools, an early childhood center, and an alternative school. Nearly 70 percent of students are Hispanic, and 100 percent of students receive free breakfast and lunch. Rouse loves her students and community and understands that most of her students are school-dependent, meaning school is more than just a place to learn reading and math—it is a safe place where they receive meals, healthcare, and counseling support.

When the pandemic hit and schools closed, she was deeply worried. Initially, her biggest concern was determining whether all students had computers and internet at home. She remembers asking herself, "How on God's green earth are we going to be able to still educate our students when they don't all have devices?"

With the help of federal ESSER funds, the district gradually managed to equip students with devices, but in the early days of remote learning, Rouse's team still scrambled to put together and deliver paper packets of instructional materials. Despite these efforts, she knew the result fell short of providing the quality education her students deserved, and it weighed on her:

> [Being a superintendent] is a calling; it's not just a job. And my calling is to make certain our kids have everything they need to be better. And here I've got them at home with a packet of paper, and nobody to instruct them or check on them. Our team stepped up, with principals delivering packets to students' homes. I knew it was the best we could do, but at the same time, what kind of education is that?

Rouse emphasized that the district could not have met the needs of students during the pandemic without significant help from the community. Even with devices for every student, the digital divide remained a challenge, and the district had to be creative in determining that students had internet access from home.

Rouse and her team distributed as many hotspots as they could to students and families, but it was not enough. There were homes that simply fell outside of cell phone range, which meant students could not attend school remotely. They provided large spaces for in-person learning at school sites with plenty of social distancing space, but even that did not fully address the need. Fortunately, they had a long-standing partnership with the local YMCA, who, prior to the pandemic, had provided before and after-school care for students. Realizing that students needed internet access to maintain connection with their teachers and classmates, the YMCA began providing all-day care where families could bring their children not just for supervision but for internet access to attend class.

Like superintendents around the country, Rouse and her team also provided students and their families with weekly meals. It became clear early on that, in some cases, these meals were the only food in the house. She recalled one particularly emotional moment when she was helping with meal distribution:

> I almost started crying. I'm handing out milk in one of the lines one day, and I'm handing a gallon into a car. All of a sudden, the kids start screaming, "Milk!" and I realized just how essential this food was for them. It was overwhelming, you know, because I knew how great the need was and that without us many of our students simply wouldn't eat. I made it clear to our staff: provide meals to any family that drives up for them. Period.

This realization was a heavy one for Rouse, and she admitted that it was hard to keep going some days. She was not alone in this struggle; the emotional responsibility for caring for their students and families in this new, remote environment is something that weighed on all superintendents, particularly those whose students were so reliant on school for their most fundamental needs.

While figuring out ways to provide students with the essentials of computer devices, internet, and food consumed much of superintendents' daily lives, addressing students' emotional well-being was equally, if not more, important during remote learning. Unlike many districts, Joliet already had social workers in all their schools, so they were able to leverage the preexisting relationships that social workers had with students and families. The social workers would check in regularly during class time, and also with their families over Zoom or the phone.

When commencement and promotion season arrived in May and June of 2020, Rouse and her team, like so many others across the country, mobilized to host drive-through (see figure 4.5) ceremonies for their eighth graders. It was far from the traditional ceremony, but it gave students the moment they had worked so hard for and gave families and staff the much-needed opportunity to celebrate.

One of the greatest challenges that emerged, however, was the difficulty in determining if students were suffering some sort of abuse or neglect since staff could not see them in person. As Rouse said, "Students don't speak their need if the person causing the need is sitting there." Teachers and school staff are mandatory reporters, meaning that if they see signs of abuse or suspect that a

Figure 4.5. Joliet Public Schools drive-through eighth-grade promotion ceremony for Washington Junior High School students in 2020. *Source*: Photo courtesy of Theresa Rouse.

student is being abused, they must report it. With schools closed, this reporting was virtually impossible. In the case of Joliet, their typical number of five to ten weekly calls to Child Protective Services dwindled to none during remote learning. Yet Rouse, like superintendents everywhere, knew that they had students who were suffering—and superintendents carried the weight of knowing there was little to nothing they could do about it. Rouse recalled one heartbreaking moment when students returned to their schools for in-person learning:

> I'll never forget the day students came back to school for the first time. I had a third grader, and she comes in the building and runs up to the first adult she sees and says, "I'm so glad to be back with you. Please help me." And she proceeds to talk about the abuse that she had been experiencing at home. But she knew she was safe there to say what she needed to say. . . . It just reconfirmed in my mind how our children were suffering, and that weight on me . . . I don't think people understand that.

Rouse's experiences underscore the multifaceted role that schools play in the lives of students, especially those from vulnerable backgrounds.

The pandemic highlighted the critical need for technology, community support, and the essential services schools provide beyond education. Rouse, her team, and the community came together to ensure that the students of Joliet Public Schools District 86 received the care and education they needed during a difficult time.

EXEMPLARY LEADERSHIP: DR. KRISTINE GILMORE ON CARING FOR STAFF

Dr. Kristine Gilmore began her tenure as superintendent in the D.C. Everest Area School District in 2003. Located in Weston, Wisconsin, the PK–12 district serves just over 6,000 students across 12 schools. Their goal is to "ensure students have the skill set to begin the next stage of their life in the 'right place'—be it a job, the military, a technical college, or four-year university." The district focuses on helping students discover their talents, interests, and suitable career paths, providing hands-on educational opportunities across academic, extracurricular, and real-world spectrums. The district also has a rich history of working collaboratively with families, community partners, and local businesses to provide students with excellent educational experiences.

Gilmore identified three main areas of focus for her and her leadership team during the pandemic: leveraging community partnerships, recognizing people and their unique situations and needs, and responding to these needs through nimble practices. What helped most in the very beginning, however, was recognizing how scary the unknown is for people. She saw that listening, empathizing, and providing reassurance were the best things she could do. Fortunately, because of who she is and how long she has been part of her community, she was uniquely equipped to do just that.

Having had her own children graduate from the district, Gilmore was a well-respected member of the community, both as a parent and superintendent. She had worked for more than two decades to build relationships and strong partnerships between local businesses and the district. She credited her deep roots as one of the things that helped her most:

> When I think about all of this, it does always comes back to community. I was blessed that I had worked for seventeen years in the community. When COVID hit, people gave us the benefit of the doubt, more often than not. Not everyone was pleased, but . . . when it came down to it, it was a community that pulled together during a difficult time to care of one another—and our kids.

Most superintendents would agree that partnering with the community, whether in a crisis situation or not, is critically important. Partnerships are built over time, however, and for those superintendents new to their jobs during the pandemic, there may have not been sufficient opportunities to establish themselves and build relationships with community leaders. The level of trust and willingness to help that Gilmore had with her community was the result of her nearly two decades in D.C. Everest. It is a reminder of how a superintendent's tenure in their district can make a difference for the students and staff they serve.

Then and now, Gilmore emphasized that being flexible is essential. Understanding that people have different experiences and needs, she worked with her team to develop options for students, staff, and families. This flexibility included providing choices between virtual and in-person learning while accommodating staff members with health concerns. Giving people options whenever she could—so they had some sense of control in a time when it was almost impossible to do so—became a hallmark of her leadership.

One of the more creative ways she provided support to her teachers was by using ESSER dollars to hire recent retirees as Building Learning Advocates. This hiring practice turned out to be a hugely successful strategy:

> We reached out to anybody who had retired within an 8- to 10-year period and told them that if they were willing to come in and help our teachers, we would make sure they stayed within the requisite hours to keep their retirement benefits, and [we would] accommodate their schedules as best we could. [So these Building Learning Advocates] would come in and do whatever teachers asked them to—following up with kids who were out for extended periods of time due to COVID and providing remedial tutoring and classroom support.

Gilmore recognized that teachers could not keep up with the needs of all their students given the extenuating circumstances that so many were facing. She and her team worked tirelessly to find creative ways to make sure that teachers felt seen and supported.

Like educators across the country, Gilmore's staff were exhausting themselves by going above and beyond to meet the needs of students, families, and community members. With the support of her board, she was able to provide $500 bonuses to staff in schools, both certificated and classified. Providing one-time bonuses to staff was a common practice in districts, but D.C. Everest took it one step further by building on and advancing their strong community ties. In addition to the bonus, staff also received $500 in gift cards because Gilmore wanted to not only support her staff but also her local business community:

> We knew that our small and local businesses were struggling, too. After board approval, my assistant and I worked with our Chamber of Commerce and picked up approximately $300,000 in gift cards in $50 increments or less because we wanted staff to spend them at a variety of businesses. I can tell you that went over so well.... Not only by our staff who felt recognized ... but also by our community and business owners who were so appreciative.

Above all else, Gilmore is someone who leads from her values, and that approach served her and her community well during the pandemic. Her commitment to providing meals for anyone who needed them is a beautiful example:

> When we were providing meals to students, we said that anybody in the community could have a meal. And we had a lot of elderly people do that because they were afraid to go to the store. [I believed] if a school can't provide a tiny meal to somebody's grandma and grandpa there's something wrong.

Under Gilmore's leadership, D.C. Everest area staff did right by their entire community, illustrating how superintendents were instrumental in supporting not just their schools, but also their broader communities when they needed it most.

INSIGHTS AND TAKEAWAYS FROM CREATING A CULTURE OF CARE

- *Schools are essential service providers.* The pandemic showed how much schools do for their students and families, in addition to teaching and learning. As Dr. Greg Baker, Superintendent of Bellingham Public Schools in Washington, said, "schools were a lifeline for their communities. In many ways, public schools bear the responsibility for leveling the playing field in our society."
- *Teachers and district leaders working as one team matters.* All too often a divide exists between school staff and district staff. During the pandemic, people pulled together, supporting not only students and families, but also one another.
- *Technology helps, but the human connection is paramount.* Technology was essential during the pandemic. Without it we would not have been able to provide any instruction or support to students. While we were grateful for it, we also learned that no technology will ever replace the in-person human connection that we all need.

While superintendents are steadfast in their commitment to educating all children, they know they cannot do so at the expense of the adults working in their systems. Compassion and care have always been fundamental in leadership, but during the pandemic, superintendents had to stay focused on their people in the midst of a multitude of pressures.

NOTES

1. Alexandrea R. Golden et al., "What Was a Gap is Now a Chasm: Remote Schooling, the Digital Divide, and Educational Inequities Resulting from the

COVID-19 Pandemic," *Current Opinion in Psychology*, June 12, 2023, https://doi.org/10.1016/j.copsyc.2023.101632.

2. Shira K. Haderlein et al., "Disparities in Educational Access in the Time of COVID: Evidence from a Nationally Representative Panel of American Families," *American Educational Research Association (AERA) Open* 7, August 23, 2021, https://doi.org/10.1177/23328584211041350.

3. USAFacts Team, "How Many US Children Receive a Free or Reduced-Price School Lunch?" *USAFacts*, October 26, 2023, https://usafacts.org/articles/how-many-us-children-receive-a-free-or-reduced-price-school-lunch/.

4. U.S. Department of Agriculture, "USDA Extends Free Meals for Kids through December 31, 2020," August 31, 2020, https://www.usda.gov/media/press-releases/2020/08/31/usda-extends-free-meals-kids-through-december-31-2020.

5. Fengxiao Li, "Impact of COVID-19 on the Lives and Mental Health of Children and Adolescents," *Frontiers in Public Health* 10 (2022), https://doi.org/10.3389/fpubh.2022.925213.

Chapter 5

Innovating to Improve Education
Teaching and Learning in New Ways

It shouldn't take a pandemic to change models of instruction that better impact student learning.

—Dr. David Miyashiro, Superintendent, Cajon Valley Union School District, California

Despite pockets of innovation, teaching and learning looked very similar before the pandemic to the ways they did a century ago. Perhaps this continuity is not a surprise. The fundamental goals of education have remained consistent from the time well before COVID-19 to the present: to ensure that students can read, write, become mathematically proficient, and think critically. Other related aims of educational leaders have similarly remained unchanged: to improve high school graduation rates, increase student engagement, see steady enrollment and consistent attendance, provide support to students with mental health issues, and raise students' overall levels of achievement.

Now, however, leaders face new realities and challenges in trying to meet these long-held goals. Along with a decline in enrollment in public schools, as figures 5.1 and 5.2 show, academic results on the National Assessment of Educational Progress (NAEP) show a decline, especially in reading and mathematics and in fourth grade. Chronic absenteeism is rising. The fact is that more students are failing and not attending school regularly. In a time of increased polarization and partisanship, marked social and cultural differences, public school educators are battling to make up for learning loss. This loss is likely due to the pandemic and a range of other factors, such as trends in homeschooling and private schools, students' fear of bullying and violence, systemic racism occurring throughout our nation's schools, more

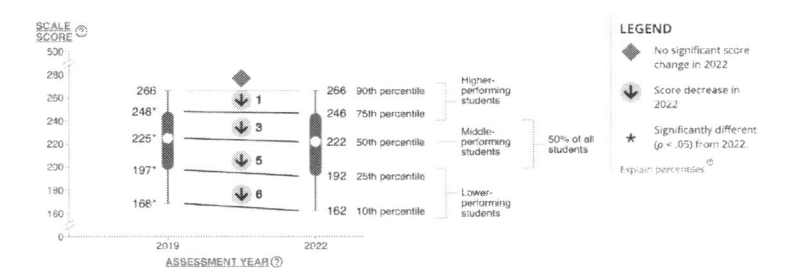

Figure 5.1. Changes in fourth-grade reading scores at five selected percentiles: 2019 and 2022. *Source:* U.S. Department of Education, Institute of Education Sciences, National Center for Education Statistics, National Assessment of Educational Progress (NAEP), 2022 Reading Assessment.

parents feeling overwhelmed, and students' feeling often disengaged and unmotivated, not seen and valued.

The importance of building strong relationships between teachers and students continues to be a cornerstone of effective education. Personal interactions, whether in-person or virtual, remain crucial for student engagement and learning. Teachers strive to create supportive and nurturing classroom environments that foster learning and personal growth while now, in many cases, also needing to address student mental health concerns exposed during the pandemic. As figure 5.3 shows, teachers, abiding by social distancing requirements and masked during the pandemic, remained committed to building and sustaining relationships with students regardless of learning modality. They adhered with dedication to the goal of keeping students connected and engaged.

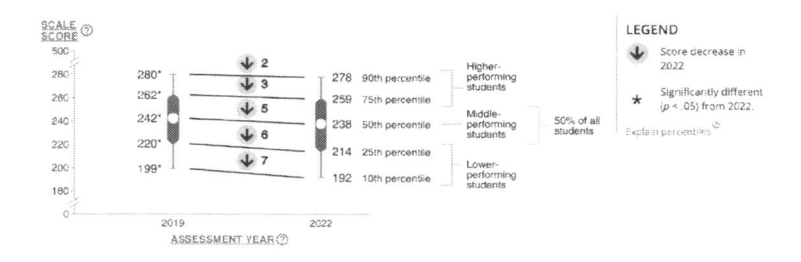

Figure 5.2. Changes in fourth-grade NAEP mathematics scores at five selected percentiles: 2019 and 2022. *Source:* U.S. Department of Education, Institute of Education Sciences, National Center for Education Statistics, National Assessment of Educational Progress (NAEP), 2022 Mathematics Assessment.

Figure 5.3. A kindergarten teacher provides outside instruction at Magnolia Elementary School during the first week of reopening school during COVID-19. *Source*: Photograph by Howard Shen, Cajon Valley Union School District, California.

TEACHING AND LEARNING PRE-COVID-19:
"Teachers were amazing in what they were able to accomplish in such a quick time."

Before the pandemic forced remote learning to quickly occur, a visitor to schools would find typical classrooms with rows of desks facing forward. The concept was to have students lined up in that grid pattern to view rigid postings of scheduled blocks of subjects, such as math, reading, and social studies, on either a chalkboard or whiteboard. Those same boards served as giant Post-it Notes to remind students to turn in homework the next day. The reminders of homework were and remain prominent, despite the research that says most homework offers minimal to no impact on student achievement.[1] While the debate over homework's value continues, research suggests that what matters most is quality assignments over quantity.[2]

The traditional school day, with its set beginning and dismissal times, often started and ended at the same times as when parents attended many years ago. The routine signaled no significant changes, even though educational experts have called for reform that supports changes to the traditional schedule. Changes that allow more time for educators to plan for better student learning include a shortened school day for students, for example, to collaboratively plan quality lessons focused on concepts for students to master, versus trying to design lessons that cover curriculum focused on quantity. When quantity over quality is chosen in lesson planning, the result is that teachers tend to focus on covering the material and pacing guides instead of the individual needs of students. When the individual needs of students are many, teachers often teach to the middle level of the class because there is not enough time to plan and differentiate the instruction for the students who either need more, less, or different instruction.

By letting go of the traditional schedule of when schools start and end, teachers are then freed up to work together and can group students differently based on mastery of skills and concepts. Planning for instruction becomes the focus of collaborative team planning, with the result that students' needs are better met. Instead of the traditional same-age grouping, different factors can be taken into account, such as how students are often at multiple age levels within a grade and they often have different learning styles. Ultimately, the time can be more effectively and efficiently used to meet more students' learning styles and educational needs. These types of flexible schedules and creative student grouping ideas were occurring in some schools, where teachers were finding the curriculum not effective in meeting the needs of students, an increase in diverse student needs, or an increase in the use of technology platforms that supported personalized learning.

Before COVID-19, educational reform advocates pushed for different learning models to allow teachers to help struggling students catch up and to address the needs of students who needed to accelerate through the curriculum. Discussions about making the shift from the traditional classroom with a teacher at the front of the room and every student on the same page of a textbook to a mastery-based approach, also known as personalized learning in elementary or secondary schools, were beginning to take shape but were hardly the norm. In secondary schools, ideas about delivering these learning models were accelerated during COVID-19 out of necessity. But prior to COVID-19, the reasons that students could potentially thrive in a nontraditional setting were that the models allowed students to work independently, meet with teachers one-on-one, and work together in small groups.

Classrooms that use personalized learning platforms and focus on mastery of concepts may mix students across age and grade levels. In a non-mastery system, students are typically provided instruction and then assessed. Once concepts are retained at or above an 80 percent level, teachers typically move on to the next concept. In a mastery-based system, students set individual goals, and once they master the concepts, they move on, getting as many attempts at the goals as they need. The traditional school calendar that consists of 180 instructional days, with its six-hour student-day seat-time requirement, is traded for competency-based hours or mastery-based graduation requirements.

There is no clear evidence that mastery learning helped students learn more or better before COVID-19. Moving forward, the unanswered questions are centered on the role technology plays in the classroom and what the right amount of screen time is, versus how seat time might be changed to incorporate some necessary changes. The aim of the changes would be to better impact student outcomes in regard to determining proficiency levels, literacy, mathematical proficiency, and critical thinking skills. Former superintendent of Fallbrook Elementary School District, Dr. Candy Singh, said:

> During the pandemic, the surge in screen time raised concerns about its impact on student's physical and mental health. In response, our teachers worked diligently to create meaningful opportunities for students to engage in learning that got them off their devices and involved in hands-on learning. Now post-pandemic, we must ensure that students, especially in the younger grades are engaged in learning experiences that promote balance and active participation beyond the screen

Many students were stressed while sitting in a classroom and were not excelling before the pandemic. Much of the anxiety that students feel comes from the pressure to perform on high-stakes tests, such as the Scholastic Aptitude Test and the American College Testing, and also from the decreased focus on the arts and other creative activities. Many students prior to the pandemic did not experience school success because of this anxiety, but also because of other factors: Teenagers often experience disruptive sleep patterns, are exposed to bullying, and are harassed by social media threats—factors that affect their well-being and education and need to be addressed.

A representative sample of American families conducted in the spring of 2020 revealed that 43 percent of parents of school-aged children said their children were less stressed when schools were closed, with only 29 percent disagreeing. Some children have been freed from bullying since schools closed. Several surveys published during the pandemic suggest that the more flexible schedules afforded by pandemic schooling are allowing teenagers to get enough sleep for the first time and that public schools, especially high schools, should take note of the flexible schedules as they reopen. In these ways, schools can better meet the needs of their students and work to address mental health issues, bullying, and the negative effects of social media on teenage behaviors.

In some respects, it was a good thing that the pandemic happened. Without the COVID-19 crisis, for example, computer device distribution and support for teachers to use different learning platforms would not have happened as quickly as they did. School districts were required to spend money on purchasing technology and the training and development to support the use of it for students and teachers. School districts were also forced to recognize the use of personalized learning platforms because that way of learning was all that could occur in some instances.

Most notably, the pandemic was a wake-up call to some about the real inequalities in student learning that teachers, principals, and superintendents got to know that have existed for a long time. The inequalities were visibly exposed daily among students who live in poverty or students who did not have access to internet service, which meant they had difficulty accessing online content. The opportunity for students to learn during COVID-19 was dependent on the basic need of getting internet service. Being able to access content became a priority, and now for students who live in poverty, it is why the research on homework finally makes sense. If students are living in cars and don't have running water or access to food, their priority at home is not completing homework. Their priority is survival.

TEACHING AND LEARNING DURING COVID-19:
"Technology is helpful, but nothing will replace a teacher."

While teachers and staff had to shift the mode in which they taught, the need to build connections with students and colleagues remained paramount during the pandemic. The priority was to provide students with engaging activities, personal connections, and opportunities for growth and achievement, even if new methods had to be quickly invented to do so. Most teachers across the country were ill-prepared as they faced the daunting task of preparing for hybrid or remote types of instruction. All at once, they needed to navigate a multitude of issues, such as developing their own technology skills, learning new pedagogies, handling student trauma remotely, and managing their own ability to understand and implement complex learning systems from home.

Districts that had invested in learning management systems (LMS) such as Canvas or Google Classroom reported being better prepared for the immediate shift to virtual classrooms than those that had not. Also, districts that had planned for one-to-one student device deployment prior to the pandemic, with careful operational management, were in a better position to support learners and the professional development of teachers throughout the pandemic.

While nearly every school district across the country attempted to deliver learning in a way that could be sustained and facilitated remotely, not every district could. Through the lens of teaching and learning, the inequities among students were exposed during the COVID-19 pandemic, especially along racial lines. Districts that worked hard to provide instructional tools, curriculum, instruction, and meals to all students across the board ran into stark inequalities that existed among students and the households where they lived. They had to confront the fact that many students lacked access to devices or broadband.

Teacher professional development was sometimes lacking, and some school districts frankly were not prepared for the massive undertaking it took to address the issues of students and staff. It was not uncommon for drive-up stations to be set up at schools or districts for families to receive devices, food, and instructional packets, all of which took a great deal of arranging to make happen. Superintendents and their leadership teams truly did whatever they needed to do to deliver whatever families needed, taking the approach that if families could not come to the schools, the schools would come to the families. Schools increasingly became community centers, providing the support that families needed to survive. To a large degree, leadership by superintendents made this remarkable outreach and adaptation possible. While principals were also instrumental in providing daily support to schools, superintendents were the ones who provided the ongoing leadership and direction to them during the pandemic.

If students were able to access instruction remotely, teachers used the most common mode of delivery, which was virtual. If not, teachers sent packets home. The benefit of the virtual classroom is that there was no need for physical space, which meant classes could occur at any time or in any geographical location.

However, virtual classrooms do not foster relationship-building. During the National Reopening Listening Tour (March 2021), Dr. Jill Biden delivered opening remarks and retold a remarkable story of a teacher who, during the height of the pandemic, chose to return to his physical classroom while his students were meeting virtually. In explaining why he made this return, the teacher said, "This is my classroom and our community, and in our classroom, we create community, take risks, build relationships, connect and form trusting bonds, and grow together." While the pandemic taught teachers and students that access is not a barrier, nothing replaces the warmth of the actual classroom. As this teacher conveyed, building community and relationships remain one of the most important things teachers do to impact student learning.

The limitations of remote teaching—and the vital importance of forming trusting in-person bonds in the live classroom—help to explain why remote learning was difficult to sustain after the COVID-19 crisis passed. As we began to emerge from the pandemic, most students did not choose to stay in full remote learning. While some students did opt for online school, many preferred face-to-face communication with teachers and peers. Above all else, most students were looking forward to going back to school because they missed their friends.

What became common when schools were closed was asynchronous learning. This model provides options for students to access and complete course materials on their own schedule, with prerecorded lessons and assignments.

In contrast, synchronous learning models use real-time online classes where teachers and students interact live through video conferencing. Some of these learning models, mainly asynchronous, have persisted post-pandemic due to their proven effectiveness and the flexibility they offer to accommodate diverse learning needs.

During the pandemic, no matter the type of instructional model, parents had a clear view of the instruction their children received, and teachers had a glimpse into the home lives of children. It was an eye-opener for parents to see the kind of instruction that teachers were delivering, as they, the parents, were often asked to help facilitate the learning at home. At the same time, teachers could see inequalities exposed in different homes, depending on economic factors, number of siblings (students were sometimes asked to help watch younger siblings, to the detriment of their own learning), lack of broadband access, and an array of other factors.

As for teachers, providing instruction during the pandemic was extremely challenging. Many were tasked with transitioning curriculum and lessons to the online format. Monitoring student engagement was difficult, with student cameras not always turned on or working properly. For teachers who were delivering instruction in schools, the challenges persisted with social distancing, Plexiglas, and contact tracing protocols to manage. Teachers did their best to focus on instruction and to manage the transitions, as students bounced back and forth from remote to in-person learning. Understandably, many found it hard to manage the stressful, confusing COVID-19 mitigation efforts on top of teaching educational content and connecting with students in meaningful ways.

TEACHING AND LEARNING POST-PANDEMIC:
"We thought we were going to ghange the entire K–12 system because of COVID-19, but we didn't."

As challenging as it was to pivot quickly and deliver instruction during COVID-19, most, if not all, superintendents were hopeful that we would apply the lessons learned from this time moving forward. The idea was that schools and leaders would return stronger, better, and more prepared to address learning loss and even permanently change the way in which educational systems deliver instruction, using a more learner-centric approach. Dr. Mary Templeton, superintendent of Washougal School District in Washington, called the expansion of learning time and technology integration, particularly techniques that assist teachers with assigning homework and monitoring instruction during the pandemic, "COVID Keepers." She said her district relies on some of the techniques and innovations that staff are determined not to abandon going forward, such as virtual meetings with parents.

Most districts invested heavily in technology, hardware and software, to support learning remotely, and they are grateful for the federal relief dollars to provide devices to students. These immediate changes, giving students access to curriculum materials and assignments 24/7, 365 days a year, are a model that most superintendents will continue if they have funds to do so. Dr. David Law, JD, is the superintendent for Minnetonka Public Schools in suburban Minnesota, and he also served during the pandemic for the largest school district in the state, Anoka-Hennepin Public Schools. He said, "The way teachers communicate with students has changed forever and for the better." As illustrated in figure 5.4, teachers are comfortable utilizing technology to enhance learning with students and, in some ways, learning alongside them. Law went on to say that one big lesson from the pandemic is:

> As much as teachers hated teaching in person and online at the same time, they got really good at it, and students have come to depend on it. Even now, when students are absent, teachers can respond that everything's on the Google Classroom, so "when you access it, if you have questions, meet me for virtual office hours for individual help."

Figure 5.4. A teacher works with Minnesota Middle School West Technology students utilizing technology during COVID-19. *Source*: Photograph courtesy of Cory Ryan, CT Ryan Photography.

The pandemic showed that technology systems can both assist with the delivery of the content and provide support when students are absent.

For many superintendents, the goal was to apply the hard lessons of the pandemic to their school systems and make necessary changes to improve teaching and learning. Districts across the country, after the pandemic, identified growing concerns for academic learning correlated with student mental and emotional health. When everyone returned to the classroom the subsequent academic year, things were worse. Dr. Gustavo Balderas, who served as superintendent in the Edmonds School District in Washington, recognized that students were not at the level they should be:

> We saw it across the board with all our students. In school's beginning weeks of kindergarten, when students gain readiness routines, some were not able to write their name, hold a pencil, or sit in a group. In the upper grades, some students struggled to regulate their outdoor behavior or were not able to perceive personal space.

That student's need prompted his district to hire more social workers and mental health support personnel for students. These compounding academic and social-emotional needs of students were not unique to Balderas's district.

The district also identified students who needed additional assistance and made recommendations for tutoring. Peer-to-peer tutoring was available three days a week after school, and additional reading teachers were hired for students who needed support. All of these supports, which continue to contribute to student growth, are now difficult to maintain given the fiscal cliff that districts face due to the sunset of pandemic-related federal funds in 2024. Families and educators have known that effective tutoring is a vital and effective tool to be continued if possible. These tutoring sessions are tailored to individual student needs, focusing on areas where students have fallen behind. Many schools are providing time for teachers to plan for small-group tutoring sessions to help students catch up on lost learning. Some districts are seeing success in growth and proficiency scores.

At the same time, we know that extended periods of remote learning and social isolation have taken a toll on students' social and emotional well-being. Supporting students' mental health requires a proactive approach on the part of district leadership teams. Recognizing the importance of mental health, districts have integrated Social Emotional Learning (SEL) into the curriculum, helping students develop resilience and cope with the emotional challenges posed by the pandemic. By focusing on these strategies, districts have mitigated the impact of learning loss and supported student recovery.

Importantly though, teachers need to be provided time to collectively meet and identify materials that students need exposure to. Teachers need time to plan their instruction focused on identified areas of need, create assessments by which to monitor instruction, and finally to collaborate as professionals to plan for paced lessons to make up for loss. Collective planning can and should be carried over into the regular school-year calendar. School districts that apply strategies to their operating plans—with a focus on flexible learning models that include extended time for teacher planning and personalized learning opportunities—will be better able to address different learning styles and student needs.

The "new normal" after the pandemic consisted of making valuable discoveries about what learning could look like. Superintendents also had to balance integrating these discoveries with the need to return to normalcy. Three big takeaways as schools returned to in-person learning after the pandemic became clear. First, the accelerated adoption of technology created a path for digital transformation that expanded access to technology, but it also highlighted equity and access disparities among students from low-income households, rural areas, and marginalized communities. Second, the rapid transition to online learning further exposed the reading and writing gaps among student groups. Many students struggle to navigate digital platforms, communicate effectively online, and critically evaluate informational resources. And third, to assist students with reading comprehension and skills for ongoing growth, teachers also require professional development to address their own digital skills gap.

It has also become clear that instruction needs to be *learner-centric*. This concept means that teachers use strategies such as personalized learning, project-based learning, and blended learning, combining both online and in-person learning. These models work to promote critical thinking, problem-solving, and collaboration skills among all students. However, the issues of equity, access, and social-emotional well-being must be addressed for these innovative practices to be sustained.

EXEMPLARY LEADERSHIP: DR. DAVID MIYASHIRO AND CAJON VALLEY UNION SCHOOL DISTRICT (CVUSD)

CVUSD serves more than 17,000 students in 27 schools in East County San Diego, California. About 69 percent of its students are from low-income households. The students are 20 percent White, 29 percent Middle Eastern/North African, 34 percent Latino, 7 percent Black, 4 percent Asian, and 6 percent Other. Before COVID-19, the district was well positioned to quickly pivot to full in-person learning just a few months after the pandemic was declared. It was a school district that was already technology rich, with a learning management system in place for its teachers and students. For years, the district had been using blended learning models that allowed for students to learn both through in-person means and from computers. Investments in one-to-one devices helped ensure students could transition to remote learning nearly seamlessly during the pandemic, especially because many students had been learning this way for years prior. The district also had the trust of its community.

When CVUSD announced that it would return to full-time in-person learning after spring break on April 12, 2020, Dr. David Miyashiro, superintendent of CVUSD, was grateful to offer in-person continuous learning opportunities for students. He was optimistic that the district could simultaneously maintain safe protocols. In addition, the school district had been working since 2014 on a blended learning model that would also help for a smooth transition to remote learning. Blended learning models are designed for students who need a more personal connection with their teacher. These models use a hybrid approach that combines online learning and traditional classroom instruction, and they emphasize personal connections between the student and teacher. The goal of blended learning models is increased student engagement and learning while supporting students' social and emotional needs. These models also allow for students to work more at their own pace.

During the pandemic, most teachers in the CVUSD observed that students had been left alone and that frustrated parents had no place to send their children for childcare. Due to the desire to provide safe places for kids to learn—established long before the pandemic—teachers embraced the opportunity to open classrooms as soon as safely possible. Within three weeks of hearing the state of California would offer a waiver for school districts that offered in-person childcare, the district began slowly opening, at first with only two classes, but by June of 2020, all twenty-seven schools were open.

What Miyashiro remembered was that this time was incredibly challenging operationally. He said, "The hardest part during that year was managing the system so that some students who chose to remain remote could, while some teachers also taught in person." The challenges were very real and unsustainable, and many believe that it contributed to educator burnout.

The CVUSD implemented several measures to address learning challenges and teacher burnout. Its aim was to ensure academic continuity during and after the pandemic. The district focused on maintaining in-person learning as much as possible, leveraging outdoor spaces, reducing class sizes, and enhancing health protocols to keep students and staff safe. They also provided after-school tutoring programs and childcare services at the beginning of the pandemic, in addition to a summer enrichment program that they continue to offer today.

The district was recognized nationally for its efforts to safely reopen and maintain continuity in learning for its students. Major factors in this success were the district's learning management system and learner-centric approach already in place, a history of trust and communication with families, and a focus on collaboration with the community, including careful listening to feedback. These factors were and are not discrete, stand-alone strengths but interwoven and mutually reinforcing, as a closer look makes clear.

CVUSD faced academic challenges like others during and after the pandemic. The district has had the typical setbacks in standardized test scores due to the disruptions in learning routines. The district is narrowing the academic gaps among students, but more work needs to be done as part of the recovery efforts to get students back to pre-pandemic levels. Statewide assessments and performance data indicated significant improvement in some students.

Miyashiro credits student mental health and wellness initiatives and other signs of progress in part to the district's communication plans with stakeholders and, in part, to their robust digital and in-person hybrid learning models. They decided to focus on communicating the importance of attending school, supporting teachers in identifying priority standards, and providing them time to plan with each other for a robust summer and extended-day student experience. They also sent a message to parents about what students need to learn to recover, resulting in a narrowing learning gap in CVUSD. The district has won praise and recognition for its efforts to reopen safely and continue to provide education to its students and basic needs to its community. The planning and forethought of its superintendent and the communication and trust established with the community were noticed and appreciated. Steps taken during the pandemic have now translated into changes in the classroom, allowing for further transformation to occur.

In the CVUSD, town halls became a way to build community trust. By March 13, 2021, over a hundred listening sessions had taken place. The session's goal was to prioritize the needs of the students and safely reopen schools. "While it can be hard to hear things at times, you need to hear those things to improve," Assistant Superintendent Karen Minshew explained during the National Safe School Reopening Summit in March 2021. Having permission to try new things became a theme for the district. Those sessions also paved a path for improved relationships between the teachers' union and district leadership.

CVUSD's vision has always been simple: Happy kids, healthy relationships, on a path to gainful employment. "When setting out to think about the vision, the thought was to keep it simple and think about what is best for kids," Assistant Superintendent Minshew said:

How we have continued to modernize education, even before COVID-19, is we use Gallup survey data to track, list priorities, and lean in on what our community is saying about our student engagement goals. A few years ago, our business community told us our focus was too narrow, and we didn't necessarily understand our student's strengths and assets.

Reviewing the national research on unemployment rates and the skills needed for gainful employment, CVUSD has worked with its teachers' union to identify student strengths, interests, and values and aligned them to their vision. The result has been increased collaboration, shared voice between leaders, consistency in expectations, and an overall increase in student outcomes.

Miyashiro attributes the district's ongoing success to collaborative planning with stakeholders but also to the robust distant learning plan it had in place prior to the pandemic. "Our first priority was to ensure meals, devices, and systems of support for those who didn't have them were in place." Certainly, having the first computer science elementary school in the country fully equipped with technology and training in place prior to the pandemic helped the district prepare for the crisis. Rios School was the first computer science elementary school in the country. Several years ago, Superintendent Miyashiro made it a priority for each of the students in the district to have a Chromebook computer. While there was already growth in the use of technology before the COVID-19 pandemic, the change was accelerated during the COVID-19 crisis. The district has continued its proactive approach and built out a twenty-year contingency plan for hardware device refresh, using ESSER funds and saving the general fund.

Miyashiro said that some of the best years of his work were during the pandemic. He feels that what he was doing during that time has changed how he leads, in part because of how he defines the role, Miyashiro reflected:

> My communication and mindset for how I approach the role has changed. I used to describe myself as an educator, but now I say, "public service provider." Being an essential worker, collaborating with the fire chief, police chief, and medical staff to pool resources to serve our families during COVID-19, meant I was right there on the frontlines with everyone else. In the past, we had men and women in uniform serving on the frontlines. They were the heroes, but after the pandemic I thought, you know, we are funded by taxpayer dollars, and we are an essential service provider.

CVUSD's ability to be one of the first districts in California to reopen came from a shared recognition between the district and their community of the need to provide essential services to families through their schools. The conversations the district held with key stakeholders included talks with health care providers, police, navy, and other professionals, who indicated that their children attended schools in the district and they needed a place to send their kids during the day. The custodial role for children that schools played during the pandemic, so parents could continue to work, was magnified.

Miyashiro and his team in CVUSD demonstrated in many ways how essential schools are and continue to be for students and families. The district is a beacon for others to learn from because of its ongoing, clear, and concise communication systems already in place prior to the pandemic. In addition, before the pandemic, the district had student advisory teams that met virtually, with a focus on student well-being and supported with grade-level curricula that had already been provided for teachers. Transitioning these delivery supports remotely was almost seamless. CVUSD continues to serve as a district others can learn from.

INSIGHTS AND TAKEAWAYS FROM INNOVATING TO IMPROVE EDUCATION

Everyone will have their own "COVID Keepers"—innovations that worked during the pandemic that can be retained to improve student outcomes. Dr. Mary Templeton, the superintendent of Washougal School District in Washington, who introduced the helpful phrase "COVID Keepers," gave an example showing how changes can lead to big improvements. "We maintain the ability to Zoom for meetings with parents who were previously required to come in for in person," she said, "like meetings for IEP (Individualized Educational Plan), an important part of the special education process. This has resulted in much better attendance."

- Include investment in long-term digital infrastructure. Ensure district growth plans focus on sustainable technology integration.
- Provide ongoing, continuous professional development for educators regarding technology platforms. Build time into the district calendar and budget to support ongoing efforts.
- Adopt comprehensive mental health programs. Advocate for integrated mental health services and social and emotional learning programs as part of the regular school curriculum.
- Build sustained family and community partnerships by fostering ongoing and proactive communication. Use virtual platforms and really listen to feedback from patrons to make changes.
- Innovate curriculum and assessment practices by developing flexible and personalized curricula. Explore alternative assessment methods that

match students' learning needs, allowing a stronger focus on learning over teaching.

Being aware of what COVID-19 keepers are, acknowledging them, and putting them into practice will create a positive legacy from a dark time.

NOTES

1. Kirsten Weir, "Is Homework a Necessary Evil?" *American Psychological Association* 47, no. 3 (2016): 36, https://www.apa.org/monitor/2016/03/homework.

2. Vicky Hallett, "Does Homework Still Have Value? A Johns Hopkins Education Expert Weighs In," Johns Hopkins University Hub, January 17, 2024, https://hub.jhu.edu/2024/01/17/are-we-assigning-too-much-homework.

Chapter 6

Communicating and Partnering with Families and Community

Ties That Bond

Why are we fighting over what books are in the library, when people are perishing over this?

—Dr. Martha Salazar-Zamora, Superintendent of
Tomball Independent School District, Texas

We all remember when school districts were delivering meals, computers, and instruction, and, in many cases, doing it outside of the normal school day. During COVID-19, districts worked tirelessly to provide these goods and services to students and parents in the community—and to communicate important information throughout the crisis.

Superintendents and their teams kept people informed, addressing a barrage of pressing questions: What were the evolving health and safety guidelines that impacted when schools would reopen? How could students access course materials while classrooms were virtual and navigate the sometimes-complicated online class schedules? Where could they pick up food? And, in some cases, what about the vaccine and its distribution? Not only did questions abound, but the correct answers often changed, then changed again.

Nonetheless, despite many uncertainties and an ever-shifting picture, the schools were resolute in helping students, families, and caregivers through the pandemic crisis. In many cities and towns across the United States, the neighborhood school became the main hub providing community support. School district superintendents were central in making this support possible, via attention to everything from large policy issues to the smallest details. And throughout, they channeled critical, timely information to those who needed it most.

Schools strive to serve families and communities, just as they strive to provide instruction to students. For school leaders, the resulting dynamics can be complex. They must grapple, for example, with how to engage families in improving student attendance and increasing public school enrollment. The basic purpose of schools, providing education to students, remains true, but the pandemic highlighted some changing or expanding roles and raised a new series of difficult questions: How do schools most effectively provide community support to families? Where do intertwined responsibilities begin and end? How can disparities best be addressed? How can everyone involve in work together to achieve the mutually held goal—the best outcome for each student, with each student reaching their full potential and being well prepared and "life-ready"?

It is not just schools reexamining their relationship with parents and families. The pandemic has changed the relationship that parents and families have with schools. Post-pandemic, many families now view schools differently. In particular, families see more clearly how the quality of education that schools provide can affect their children's future, for better or worse. This perspective has contributed to the school choice movement and can be traced back, in part, to the difference in how families interacted with schools during the pandemic. It is no longer the norm for children to wake up early, catch the school bus, go to school, and return home. Now, with virtual learning opportunities, flexible learning schedules, and many ways to address a variety of family and student needs, families have come to expect more choices beyond the traditional public school learning day. The pandemic brought out culture wars and malaise in education, and the media focused on the exasperation that some families were experiencing with schools.

As families explored alternative options for their children's education, superintendents were under increased pressure to work with schools to seek innovative solutions and partner with families to meet their needs. It was difficult to establish and maintain relationships with families who expected something different from schools when those schools were just trying to open their doors and get things back to normal. Former superintendent Matt Miller expressed the difficulty:

> We were facing staffing shortages, technology and infrastructure challenges, and still dealing with COVID cases, so while we wanted to be innovative and keep classes online with flexible start and end times, it was oftentimes not possible because we didn't have the staff. Some parents understood that, and some didn't.

How schools respond to the changing needs of families and to the changing needs of communities will directly impact the future of the nation's public school enrollment. Furthermore, how schools and school districts improve and adapt to communication expectations from families will also impact the future of public schools in the United States.

SCHOOLS' AND PARENTS' RELATIONSHIPS CHANGED:
"How I view school now will never be the same."

Although the pandemic changed many factors about how schools and families interrelate, one thing has not changed: to be learning at a rate commensurate with their peers, most students need to be in school. But when the pandemic forced closures, schools, students, and families were forced to work together in a more coordinated effort. This effort manifested itself in unique ways, both inside and outside of the classroom.

With schools closed, parents and families were forced to assume an expanded role in the education of their children. Formerly, in collaboration with the school, parents and families looked after the interests and success of their students, with the schools providing the bulk of the formal, day-to-day instruction. During the pandemic, a new role for parents and families became more active and involved in the daily activities of teaching. In some cases, parents had to almost become teachers and learning facilitators, with limited training in how to do so.

The essential role of families in the teaching and learning process was clear before the pandemic. Research has shown that the level of family involvement in schools is one of the main drivers in determining the success or failure of educational systems.[1] The pandemic revealed that many other needs also had to be addressed, in addition to differences in the level of family involvement. And it shone a light on interrelated disparities that existed—in economic resources, internet accessibility, digital skills, and the abilities of families to provide curricular help.

The pandemic highlighted the interdependence between families, students, and schools. Schools were forced to establish a different kind of relationship with families, who assumed the role of co-teacher, and students were asked to continue developing skills independently as they worked to understand new learning platforms. Families had to internally strengthen relationships with their children for optimal educational success.

A perennial challenge for the school districts has always been how to engage with families in meaningful ways. Despite their best efforts, many teachers have called for more robust connections and greater involvement from all educational community members. Parental involvement in education has always been considered essential to children's school performance. Children may internalize the value over time so that they are autonomously motivated in academics, which ultimately heightens their engagement in school.[2]

Through their involvement, parents may also increase children's experience with academic activities, thereby leading children to view themselves as academically competent.[3] As parents converted their homes into classrooms, the pandemic presented an opportunity for parents to learn new skills along with students. Among the most challenging aspects of the pandemic that families expressed were feelings of frustration, concern, and denial while parents tried to combine housework with homework; dealt with the need to create or establish communication links with teachers to guarantee educational tutoring for their children; and managed and balanced the time spent on educational needs with their needs to work either outside the home or work from home.

School districts that worked on centralizing communication strategies helped to alleviate some of the stress parents felt and also reduced the work of teachers. Dr. Scott A. Menzel, superintendent of Scottsdale Unified School District, said that during the pandemic,

> We created a centralized communications team that was responsible for ensuring teacher links worked. The relevant expertise came from the teachers, but the "comms team" uploaded the information and presented the content in a clear and concise way, to help with the workload of the teachers. When districts send messages to parents every one to three days, regardless of whether it is during a pandemic or not, parents get used to that kind of consistent messaging, and it helps build trust with them.

A key change during the pandemic was the fact that parents were often able to provide feedback from their makeshift school environments during the time classroom instruction was delivered. That change helped families feel that they were listened to and supported in their new role as co-teachers. They were acting as a facilitator, or co-teacher, in real time. Because teachers would respond via chat rooms, it was as if the parent or caregiver were in the classroom, learning right along with their child.

During virtual community meetings, school leaders discussed mitigation plans for reopening and solicited feedback from community members and families, viewing them as vital partners in the process. Superintendents provided daily informational briefings to parents and community members through a variety of platforms. Facebook Live, for example, was used to ensure that the community saw superintendents working through the mitigation plans, addressing concerns, and answering questions. This transparency helped to earn and maintain trust with community members.

The meetings were as much about information sharing as they were about asking for feedback. Superintendents also worked through the timelines to spend federal relief dollars, to safely reopen, and to plan effective strategies for addressing learning loss. Dr. Carrie Stephenson, superintendent of Montrose County School District in Colorado, said, "We had direct contact with parents through our student information system. Teachers used technology methods such as Google Classroom, Class Dojo, etc. And we updated our website frequently."

BUILDING TRUST WITH FAMILIES:
"People see me as a human, and not just a name who signs the back-to-school letter, now."

The pandemic changed the way many families and students feel about school, just as it changed the way many employees feel about going to work. A growing preference for a hybrid schedule, a desire to flex hours, and a pull to work from home have changed the way students and families view schooling. Some have a desire for a flexible structure that matches the schedule of what the pandemic brought to people who go to work. Other parents were inspired to seek a different option other than public schools, like charter schools, micro schools, and private or home schooling. These trends are part of the reason that public school enrollment has declined since the pandemic. In the four years since the pandemic closed schools, U.S. education has struggled to recover to pre-pandemic enrollment numbers. Just as concerning is the high number of students who are now chronically absent from school, as attendance rates fall lower.[4]

Addressing the importance of school attendance needs to be as urgent as the need to provide food and medical services and information about class assignments during the pandemic. Superintendents were and remain committed to their communities, determined that students would receive food and access to instruction and that parents would know details about when schools would open and close and what services would be available on a daily, sometimes twice-daily basis. If the widespread problems with attendance are going to be addressed, the same effective, concerted communication strategies deployed during COVID-19 must be applied with just as much urgency.

CHRONIC ATTENDANCE WORSENS, POST-PANDEMIC:
"We are still trying to locate lost students."

During the 2020–2021 school year, at least 14.7 million students nationwide were chronically absent.[5] Chronic absenteeism among K–12 students had almost doubled from more than 8 million students pre-COVID-19, who were missing 10 percent or more of school days due to absence for any reason—excused, unexcused absences, and suspensions. Those missed days can translate into students having difficulty learning to read by the third grade, achieving in middle school, and graduating from high school.

In 2022, after the pandemic, the percentage of students classified as chronically absent from school drastically increased to an estimated 26 percent, according to the most recent data from forty states and Washington, D.C., compiled by the conservative-leaning American Enterprise Institute.[6] Small declines in the number of absent students in 2023 have not eased concerns about the problem. Even pre-pandemic, chronic absenteeism rates among students were already alarming. To make matters more challenging, chronic absenteeism rates among Black and Hispanic students are the highest, and those in high-poverty districts are often the students who have the most learning loss to make up.

Children living in poverty are two to three times more likely to be chronically absent—and they face the most harm because their community lacks the resources to make up for the lost learning in school. It is interesting to note that English learners, who face significant barriers in school and society, are approximately 1.2 times less likely to be chronically absent than their non-English-learner peers. The same is not true for students with disabilities, who are 1.5 times more likely to be chronically absent than students without disabilities.

Chronic absenteeism is not simply a matter of truancy or skipping school. In fact, many of these absences, especially among our youngest students, are excused. Often, absences are tied to health problems such as asthma, diabetes, and mental health issues. Other barriers that can make it difficult to go to school every day include the lack of a nearby school bus, no safe route to school, or food insecurity. In many cases, chronic absences go unnoticed because schools are counting how many students show up every day rather than examining how many and which students miss so much school that they are falling behind.[7]

Some pre-pandemic initiatives have been successful in reducing absenteeism. These included low-cost interventions such as communication efforts and more expensive ones such as transportation and staffing for counselors. Whether and how much pandemic-era interventions work to address chronic absenteeism is yet to be known. Regardless of the cost or type of intervention, schools typically are not looking enough on identifying and addressing the underlying causes. Schools tend to treat the absences with a punitive response, as opposed to looking at the root causes of the issue. Menzel has worked to reverse this response:

> Our district focuses on the root causes because we value the relationships between the teacher and student and know that—by changing the narrative from "you've missed so many days, so you are now suspended" to "let's find out why

you are staying home"—through our human connection we have a better chance of getting the students to stay in school.

The reality, Menzel said, is that COVID-19 changed the way parents and kids feel about going to work and school. On the positive side, he said:

> We appreciate that when people are sick, they stay home, and we also value the fact that mental health days are in place. I just think we really need to work on creating safe and respective learning environments where kids feel safe, seen, and heard.

He described his district's attendance task force that is working to create an engaging curriculum and "spaces where kids like to be." Ideally, he said, kids should be "begging to be at school—you know, #FOMO: fear of missing out."

Some of the root causes of absenteeism, however, can be attributed to the pandemic. The pandemic caused a disruption to the routine of going to school every day. It also made it seem as though missing a day of school was less important than it used to be. During the pandemic, the upheaval in school routines eroded the traditional expectations for attendance, creating new habits for students and families. The spike in chronic absenteeism during the pandemic might not fully explain this shift, but the persistence of high absentee rates afterward does highlight a lasting change in cultural norms.

The habit of daily attendance and many families' trust were both severed when schools shuttered in spring 2020. Even after schools reopened (from August 2020 to the spring of 2021), things did not snap back to normal. School districts offered remote options, required COVID-19 quarantines, and relaxed policies around attendance. This cultural shift is making it difficult for schools to expect parents and students to revert to the traditional routine of going to school every day. And students do not want to forego the luxury of using remote and blended learning models, such as Zoom, Canva, and Google Classroom if they miss school. Because of their experiences during the COVID-19 pandemic, some parents and students are seeking, for example, state-sponsored vouchers for alternative education options other than public schools.

Before the COVID-19 pandemic, family involvement in education was increasing in some schools, fostering a more collaborative relationship between teachers and families. This growing engagement was evident through initiatives like student-led conferences, various volunteering opportunities both in and out of school, and the recognition of families as valuable contributors to student learning. Some districts were engaging technology to host student-led meetings, virtual parent meetings, and staff meetings (and were thankful those platforms were in place during the pandemic for feedback and to maintain relationships between students, teachers, and parents). These types of activities encouraged trust, engagement, and a true partnership between schools and parents.

Not lost in the moment is the fact that some families, even before COVID-19, did not always feel welcome to participate in the traditional ways offered by schools. Traditional activities such as volunteering in schools, parent-teacher conferences, and parent committees have not always been available to families from low socioeconomic backgrounds and are often reflected in low participation rates in schools. Sometimes teachers or staff will inappropriately confuse the families' low participation rates in traditional school-led activities for a lack of interest in their child's education.

The rapid shift to virtual classrooms during the pandemic helped change this perception and increase parent and family engagement. Families instantly, in "real time," saw what was occurring in classrooms and were able to provide feedback and, in some cases, asked to help deliver instruction. In some ways, teachers gained a new understanding of what home life looked like for many students. Kindergarten teachers were amazed that moms and dads, for example, had classrooms set up in kitchens, bedrooms, and living rooms. If the family had both parents working remotely from home and three young children and two teenagers working remotely in the rooms of the home, it was at times chaotic—but they were making it work.

Before COVID-19, the normal communication pattern would likely have been for the parent to send an email or make a phone call to the teacher if a concern arose with something going on with the child's instruction. During COVID-19, however, the parent was able to join the teacher in a breakout office room with the student, discuss the matter, and receive an answer. When the pandemic ended and schools reopened, some teachers did not keep the same close and relatively easy communication patterns in place with families, so the frequency of interactions diminished. At times, parents weren't welcomed back into the classroom as frequently as they once were, even before COVID-19.

Gallup asked respondents for their views of K–12 education on a four-point scale, ranging from completely satisfied to completely dissatisfied. In 2023, 9 percent of Americans were completely satisfied with U.S. public schools, while 32 percent of parents indicated they were somewhat dissatisfied.[8] In light of these sobering figures, schools partnering with communities and families in fresh and innovative ways gives school districts an opportunity to change perceptions about schools post-pandemic. Although teachers and parents were given significant grace during the pandemic, some of the most divisive, angry, and mistrustful exchanges occurred between families and schools at the height of the pandemic. As noted earlier, research shows that when schools have strong relationships with families, students perform better. They are more likely to stay in school, graduate, and do well academically.

PARENTS ARE THEIR CHILDREN'S FIRST TEACHER:
"Engaging families as partners—one of the silver linings of the madness."

COVID-19 relief funding provided a unique opportunity to rebuild public education after exceptionally challenging years. As CEO of Successful Practices Network, Bill Daggett, and former executive director of AASA, Dan Domenech, have argued, we need to "rethink families, students, and communities as co-authors of education," rather than conceptualizing families as the recipients of services or, even worse, as barriers to implementation.

In an *EdWeek* Research Center survey last summer, 50 percent of educators said they expected insufficient parent engagement to pose a major challenge in the 2023–2024 school year.[9] But are parents sufficiently engaged and knowledgeable about how their children are doing? Gallup and Learning Heroes, a nonprofit organization that works on expanding family partnerships with schools, found that parents largely misunderstand their children's academic performance. In the survey, 88 percent of parents said their children were at or above grade level in reading, and 89 percent believed the same for math.[10] In fact, on the 2022 National Assessment of Educational Progress, only a quarter of fourth-grade students and 38 percent of eighth-grade students met basic benchmarks in math. In reading, 37 percent of fourth graders and 30 percent of eighth graders did.[11]

Related to the picture that emerges of parents being out of touch with educational realities, *Education Next* noted that 43 percent of parents report that their children did not experience any learning losses during the pandemic.[12] These results are worrisome to educators, in part because the results do not comport with researchers' understanding of the breadth and magnitude of pandemic harm on test score growth.

When watching their children engage in remote learning, with the rapid Zooming from one class to the next, many families had voiced concerns over virtual classrooms being less effective than live classrooms. However, what is troubling is this fact: in 2022, only 9 percent of parents said they are not confident their child will "catch up" from COVID-related learning loss within a year or two. The rest are either confident the child will catch up (49 percent of parents feel their children will catch up) or they perceive no learning loss in the first place (43 percent of parents perceive no learning loss in their children in the first place).[13] The reality is that even before the pandemic, some students had tremendous gaps in learning. After the pandemic, the gaps were widened, and parents were under the impression that sooner or later (even without targeted support) most students would catch up. Superintendents found this response to be troubling.

Schools don't necessarily need a significant increase in funding or a specialized staff position, such as a family engagement counselor, to bridge the perception gap. Instead, it requires a change in mindset among school staff to focus on fostering partnerships with families and involving parents and caregivers in discussions about academic achievement and student well-being. With students' literacy and math skills declining to unprecedented levels, many schools will need to understand how to make this partnership a priority.

Valuing families within the school environment is essential for building strong relationships among teachers, students, student support staff, and the families raising these children. In the wake of COVID-19, with students exhibiting increased social and emotional wellness needs, it was, and remains particularly beneficial to involve families in discussions and planning related to their children's education. Engaging families in school learning, planning, and activities not only fosters positive family involvement but also enhances overall student success, reinforcing the importance educators place on family participation.

When schools and classrooms develop integrated plans to include families in educational experiences, future educators gain a better understanding and appreciation of the family's role in education. During COVID-19, we saw an increased interdependence between the teacher and the caregiver, each relying on the other to assist with the child's learning. Superintendent Dr. Deborah Kerr, St. Francis Public School District, Wisconsin, highlighted this fact:

> What has been difficult is that once schools decided to reopen, after promptly closing virtual classrooms, it eliminated a parent's access to their child's on-demand virtual activity. And at the same time, it also eliminated that frequent ongoing communication that parents came to rely on.

The same kind of openness between teacher and parent left many families feeling shut out when the pandemic ended. Making matters worse, some districts tightened up protocols, limiting outside visitors to schools during the initial reopening phases. During those first few months, it was challenging to transition from virtual classrooms to in-person learning and at the same time try to maintain a new sense of reciprocal relationships between caregiver and educator. As Kerr expressed,

> When parents engage with you, and you feel that sense of trust, they feel like they have some of that control as you are planning with them. To build

partnerships, to connect with other families, you can build a stronger community than if you just have the administration try to do all of it.

FINDING NEW WAYS TO COMMUNICATE:
"I am amazed at the hits that videos get, so now I rely on them, versus the letter."

"Communications was at the forefront during the pandemic, driving forward key policies that now influence the way we work," said Dr. Martha Salazar-Zamora, superintendent of Tomball Independent School District (ISD) in Texas.

> My biggest fear at the time was that I wouldn't be able to take away the fear or lack of fear that parents had about sending their children to school. I wanted them to hear from me, that their children were safe when they were with us.

The way superintendents had to communicate with families and their communities changed during the pandemic. "I used to always write a traditional back-to-school or end-of-school letter, but now I do a virtual video," Salazar-Zamora said. "I am just amazed at the number of hits that those get. I don't know how many people were reading my back-to-school or end-of-year letter, but I know they watch the videos."

Overcommunication, borne out of necessity during COVID-19, is now the expectation for many families. Salazar-Zamora explained that school districts are viewed in many communities as businesses, with all the related communication expectations:

> We are often the largest employers, and employers are businesses with large budgets, and a business communicates. We ensure that our business—that is, the school district—communicates information through all its social media platforms—and not just the celebratory kind [of information], like who won Friday night's football game, but other educational information."

She feels it is necessary to communicate in this frequent, accessible way to keep the community connected and engaged in the business of the district.

Intentional face-to-face opportunities have made the community feel more connected to her. She said,

> I'll see someone in the grocery store now, and they'll say hi. I know they feel like they know me because they have seen my face and heard my voice. It makes me more relatable. Whereas before, my name along with three degrees behind it was just a name signed on a piece of paper.

In essence, the superintendent is not an intimidating person that parents and families cannot relate to—no longer just someone who makes big decisions and is rarely seen, except at high school graduations or other public speaking events.

TEAMWORK IN PLANNING THE JOHN S. MCCAIN III ELEMENTARY SCHOOL:
"We were focused on the future."

Never had an elementary school been named after the late senator, John S. McCain, but in July of 2021, after an aggressive nine-month construction schedule during COVID-19, the John S. McCain (JSM) school opened in Buckeye, Arizona. Throughout its planning, a superintendent, in this case, Dr. Kristi Wilson, together with a diverse group of community members, had challenged themselves with key questions: How could a school be designed differently, with the characteristics of the late senator in mind? How could the school place project-based learning at its center and offer its students computer science immersion as an educational program and curriculum? How could the community also gain benefits from the building for adult teaching and learning purposes? And what would students need to know to be prepared for the unknown future?

Both the challenges and opportunities were massive. The community had recently passed a bond allocating the money needed to build the school. Most school buildings in the district were traditionally constructed with brick walls and standard rows of desks and did not offer a forward-looking computer science immersion program. But it was imperative for the planning team to proceed and "think outside the box," in part to compete with the school choice movement that was starting to take over from the eastern section of Maricopa County. The task of reimagining and rethinking how new educational spaces and curriculum could work would take many meetings and conversations over the twelve-month planning phase prior to COVID-19.

During the meetings between community stakeholders and the district administration team, trust grew and bonds formed. Community representatives included the mayor, the fire chief, city hall officials, principals, parents, teachers, students, support staff, clergy, bus drivers, business owners, and governing board members. People brought their own unique perspectives and were encouraged to engage and share ideas and opinions. Participants observed a range of K–12 educational spaces that were built with the vision of something different and workable. Throughout this planning phase, the overarching goal of the meetings was to figure out ways to make JSM a place where students would not be restricted by a dated architectural style and where they could engage with their education in learner-centric ways.

Because there are not many places in the city of Buckeye for groups to meet, the stakeholders also thought with intensity and creativity about how JSM could benefit the citizens as well as its students—how the community as a whole could take advantage of the school's technology and meeting spaces, designed for learners. The school presented a great opportunity to help people to incorporate technology into their daily lives and, as importantly, help them see how changes in technology can be manifested in the classroom. Architects brought in conceptual drawings and furniture manipulatives so participants could see and feel how classrooms, hallways, and professional learning spaces could work together in new and different ways, with learners in mind.

One result was a "learning stair." This architectural feature was prominently placed in front of a media wall upon the entrance of the school. It was something new to the district, providing a place for students to both create and collaborate and also providing members of the community innovative opportunities for professional development and meetings, as seen in figure 6.1. The idea was that after school and in the evenings, parents and community members would also utilize the learning stair and media wall to

Figure 6.1. John S. McCain Elementary School learning stair and digital computer screen. *Source*: Photograph courtesy of Patrick Sheppard, Chasse Construction Company.

collaborate and communicate. While holding meetings or showcasing current events, they would find the technology in the media wall useful, similar to how students were using it and learning in school.

When COVID-19 hit, the team that was working to plan and design the school had to shift promptly to a schedule of virtual meetings. They pivoted to using technology, including artificial intelligence (AI), to see renderings of the building. Some of the stakeholders shared that if it weren't for their commitment to the building of the John S. McCain School, they doubted they would have advanced their technology skills as far as they did. They appreciated the opportunity to learn the new technology. Many participants of the school's design team also noted that while, at first, they were skeptical of (or closed off to) innovative ideas—such as retractable glass walls, movable furniture in classrooms, and roaming carts instead of teachers' desks—now they could see the rationale behind these and other changes. Because of the communication techniques and engagement strategies used during the planning meetings, they now understood and supported the changes—and applauded them.

To be clear, naming the school after John S. McCain was purposeful. The senator was known for his character and his admirable traits of being able to compromise, work collaboratively with others, and put service above self. These qualities were touchstones for leadership, embedded in the character program throughout the curriculum at the school. As seen in figure 6.2, the main entrance of the school features an image of John S. McCain and the words of his farewell speech, which he delivered from the Arizona State Senate in 2018. It is here where students in all K–8 grade levels can engage in the school's signature computer science programmatic aspects but also can learn the traits the late senator stood for. Terms like "courage," "honor," "service," and "collaboration" are vividly displayed on the school's entrance wall. Students learn how those traits will help them to succeed in school and in life and how to work together. Teachers are encouraged to incorporate lessons that help students learn what the terms mean, as they all work with each other and develop a new skill and language like computer science.

The school's physical building is like no other in the district. JSM has no internal classroom brick walls. The classroom's walls are all glass. This change has many benefits, such as when teachers need to schedule intervention groups (focused teaching sessions for students who need some extra help and time). Instead of having these groups meet within the walls of their own classes, teachers are now able to provide space for small groups to receive extra instruction that can occur nearby. The groups can take place between and among kids in different ability groups without the barriers of walls, as illustrated in figure 6.3. It took a lot of planning and understanding on the part

Communicating and Partnering with Families and Community 99

Figure 6.2. The late Senator John S. McCain's farewell speech is displayed on his image on the interior wall of the elementary school named after him in Buckeye, Arizona.
Source: Photograph courtesy of Vispi Karanjia, Orcutt Winslow Architects.

Figure 6.3. Superintendent Wilson looks on as a student is working in the hallway, illustrating the small-group setting design aspect of John S. McCain Elementary School.
Source: Photograph courtesy of Kristi Wilson.

of teachers to see how this different model could help students of different ability levels perform better, and for the community to get behind the concept for it to work.

Similarly, the educational program is unlike others in the district, in that the curriculum centers on computer science immersion. The school has a full-capacity enrollment of 800 students. Student instruction in computer science is required for all K–8 students who attend JSM. Kindergarten students are writing code as they simultaneously learn to sound out letters, write their names, count to ten, play a musical instrument in band, or learn to jump rope in physical education class. Along with learning the basics of reading, writing, and arithmetic, all kindergarten through eighth-grade students, for example, also design robots that can follow basic instructions. Students write the code that the robots follow, and eighth graders build robots that are entered into statewide competitions. In these and other ways, school districts, principals, and teachers are working to make instruction personal, relevant, and meaningful to students.

When the pandemic hit, the planning process and the whole project itself could have lost momentum. Because trust and good channels of communication had already formed, however, and a strong rationale and purpose had been established, JSM was built on time and under budget. It truly displayed what anthropologist Margaret Mead meant when she said, "Never doubt that a small group of thoughtful, committed citizens can change the world. Indeed, it is the only thing that ever has." Individuals involved in this ambitious community-based process can truly take pride in having helped to create a school that will serve thousands of students for hundreds of years.

In the book *On Call* (2024), Anthony Fauci wrote, "A leader, particularly in an area of controversy, cannot make everyone happy all the time. If you do, you are probably not a good leader and you soon will not be respected."[14] Given the high level of innovation in the project and its size, budget, and schedule, it was impossible to please everyone, meet everyone's needs, and answer everyone's questions in a way that satisfied all. But it was clear that by focusing on the unknown future—and on the job of building spaces for students with the future in mind—the outcome would be positive, and it is. One thing that was learned from building this school, John S. McCain, during COVID and opening after COVID, *was the power of communicating and partnering with families and community members*. The content of the communication may have been controversial and, at times, not what people wanted to hear or agreed with, but there was time to process and consider information as the basis for decision-making, time to air ideas and talk, and, overall, a shared purpose.

EXEMPLARY LEADERSHIP: DR. MARTHA SALAZAR-ZAMORA, THE "ENTERPRISE SUPERINTENDENT" OF TOMBALL ISD, DESTINATION DISTRICT, TEXAS

Coming out of COVID-19, Tomball ISD in Texas created an Academy of Energy and International Business, the first in the state. The idea was for students to spend their high school years learning in a facility different from the traditional high school. However, to the surprise of Salazar-Zamora, she received a bankruptcy notice from the oil and gas company that was a primary partner of the innovative concept. The dream of opening the Academy would be put on hold until she could secure another facility. What Salazar-Zamora did next, however, was capitalize on her ability to generate funds for her district. She calls herself an enterprise superintendent because of this ability.

Salazar-Zamora knew she had to work diligently and quickly to enlist other oil and gas partners to secure a space to house hundreds of high school-aged students, but no appropriate facilities were available. Then, on her daily commute to and from work, the superintendent noticed a "For Sale" sign posted on the same building from which she had received a bankruptcy notice. She saw this sign as an opportunity to purchase, and she worked with her finance team to purchase a 70-acre space with ten buildings. In this way, she was able to establish the Tomball Innovation Center, which offers career and college growth opportunities for students.

The district also rents a portion of the building to help fund support services for career and technology-based activities that support the center. "A facility that is today worth four hundred million dollars, I purchased for thirty-nine million dollars. I rent out part of the building and utilize the dollars impacting our Career and Technical Education (CTE) Programs." Those programs include pilot mechanic programs, a full court where students interested in the law can observe lawyers and judges in mock trials, 911 safety simulation programs, cybersecurity, drone development, and several other career-related programs that match student and community needs.

Working with the community, Salazar-Zamora has secured grants and other community donations to further develop programs. These programs help support high school students in pursuing careers that interest them and that are likely to lead to good job opportunities. The district's partnership with the Texas Education Agency (TEA)—and their Pathways in Technology Early College High Schools (P-TECH) initiative—offers an open-enrollment program that creates workforce pathways aligned with high-demand, high-wage fields throughout the state. Students enrolled in the P-TECH program work toward an associate's degree while gaining hands-on work experience,

Figure 6.4. Students enrolled in the P-TECH program at the Tomball Innovation Center gain knowledge, skills, and dispositions that prepare them for the world of work.
Source: Photograph courtesy of Allison Suarez, Tomball ISD.

as seen in figure 6.4. The program focuses on providing opportunities for high school students to earn associate degrees and for paraprofessionals to earn a bachelor's degree in education. The paraprofessional education preparation programs come with the stipulation that credits will be paid for with a three-year commitment to work in the Tomball ISD.

The Academy for Energy and International Business is still in the making at Tomball ISD. When Tomball ISD purchased the facility from the oil and gas company, Salazar-Zamora worked to secure lease options with other local oil and gas companies to utilize unused portions of the facility, while the district works to develop Career and Technical Education (CTE) programs housed on the property. She is currently working with district leaders to put the final programmatic touches with the goal of opening the Academy soon. The dream of working with business partners to improve outcomes for students is being fulfilled one day at a time in Tomball ISD. Sparked by the innovative spirit of an entrepreneurial superintendent, Tomball Innovative Center supports students in their pursuit of learning connected to careers. The developments that are proceeding have kept families and the community engaged and optimistic.

INSIGHTS AND TAKEAWAYS ON COMMUNICATING AND PARTNERING WITH FAMILIES AND COMMUNITY

- Clear, concise, and consistent communication messaging from the superintendent was what families and the community members came to rely on during COVID-19. Remembering these three Cs of communication strategy will be important as superintendents venture into a new era of relationships between schools and families.
- Prioritize student attendance and engagement. Work with teachers and principals to identify and eliminate the root causes of chronic absenteeism within school systems.
- Reach out to stakeholders in the community to make reducing chronic absenteeism a broadly owned and widely shared civic priority. Enlist families, civic and elected leaders, local businesses, and clergy members in the call to engage students in learning and to identify and develop solutions to attendance barriers.
- If an opportunity presents itself to build a new school or to redesign an educational space, involve the community and students so all affected will have FOMO (fear of missing out) and will want to be there every day.
- Partner with other innovative superintendents who are finding ways to innovate. Engage with the community in new ways, encouraging connection. Whether you have an opportunity to expand CTE programs or collaborate on projects, prioritize finding of new ways to engage students and families. Keep in mind the goal of using educational spaces and programs differently, with an eye toward the future.

As John McCain said, "In America, we change things that need to be changed. Each generation makes its contribution to our greatness. The work that is ours to do is plainly before us; we don't need to search for it." And as

Abraham Lincoln expressed, "If we never try, we shall never succeed," and "You cannot fail, if you resolutely determine that you will not."

NOTES

1. Michael M. Barger et al., "The Relation between Parents' Involvement in Children's Schooling and Children's Adjustment: A Meta-Analysis," *Psychological Bulletin* 145, no. 9 (2019): 855–90, https://doi.org/10.1037/bul0000201.

2. Cecilia Sin-Sze Cheung and Eva M. Pomerantz, "Why Does Parents' Involvement Enhance Children's Achievement? The Role of Parent-Oriented Motivation," *Journal of Educational Psychology* 104, no. 3 (2012): 820–32, https://doi.org/10.1037/a0027183; Wendy S. Grolnick and Maria L. Slowiaczek, "Parents' Involvement in Children's Schooling: A Multidimensional Conceptualization and Motivational Model," *Child Development* 65, no. 1 (1994): 237–52, https://doi.org/10.2307/1131378.

3. Eric Dearing et al., "The Promotive Effects of Family Educational Involvement for Low-Income Children's Literacy," *Journal of School Psychology* 42, no. 6 (2004): 445–60, http://doi.org/10.1016/j.jsp.2004.07.002; Grolnick and Slowiaczek, "Parents' Involvement"; Sehee Hong and Hsiu-Zu Ho, "Direct and Indirect Longitudinal Effects of Parental Involvement on Student Achievement: Second-Order Latent Growth Modeling across Ethnic Groups," *Journal of Educational Psychology* 97, no. 1 (2005): 32–42, https://doi.org/10.1037/0022–0663.97.1.32.

4. "Chronic Absenteeism in the Nation's Schools: A Hidden Educational Crisis," U.S. Department of Education, June 2016, updated January 2019, https://www.2.ed.gov/datastory/chronicabsenteeism.html.

5. "Chronic Absence," Attendance Works, https://www.attendanceworks.org/chronic-absence/the-problem.

6. Nat Malkus, "Long COVID for Public Schools: Chronic Absenteeism before and after the Pandemic," American Enterprise Institute, January 31, 2024, https://www.aei.org/research-products/report/long-covid-for-public-schools-chronic-absenteeism-before-and-after-the-pandemic/.

7. "What's the Difference between Chronic Absence and Truancy?" Attendance Works, January 11, 2016, https://www.attendanceworks.org/whats-the-difference-between-chronic-absence-and-truancy/.

8. Lydia Saad, "Americans' Satisfaction with K–12 Education on Low Side," *Gallup*, September 1, 2022, https://news.gallup.com/poll/399731/americans-satisfaction-education-low-side.aspx.

9. Libby Stanford, "What the Parents' Rights Movement Forced Schools to Do," *Education Week*, April 25, 2024, https://www.edweek.org/leadership/what-the-parents-rights-movement-forced-schools-to-do/2024/04.

10. Gallup and Learning Heroes, "B-flation: How Good Grades Can Sideline Parents," 2023, p. 4, https://bealearninghero.org/wp-content/uploads/2023/11/B-flation_Gallup_Learning-Heroes_Report-FINAL.pdf.

11. "Thirty-three Percent of Fourth-Graders at or above NAEP Proficient in Reading, Lower Compared to 2019," NAEP Report Card: Reading 2022, https://www.nationsreportcard.gov/reading/nation/achievement/?grade=4.

12. Paul E. Peterson, David M. Houston, and Martin R. West, "Parental Anxieties over Student Learning Dissipate as Schools Relax Anti-Covid Measures," *Education Next*, Winter 2023, https://www.educationnext.org/wp-content/uploads/2022/12/ednext_XXIII_1_ednext_parent_survey.pdf.

13. Peterson, Houston, and West, "Parental Anxieties."

14. Anthony Fauci, *On Call: A Doctor's Journey in Public Service* (New York: Viking, 2024), 67.

Chapter 7

Managing Politics While Prioritizing Students

Your politics is tethered to the level of advocacy you're willing to demonstrate.

—Dr. Baron Davis, former Superintendent,
Richland School District Two, South Carolina

The role of the superintendent has always been a political one. Some say it is one of the most political positions a person can hold without running for elected office, and the pandemic and the rise of hyper-partisan politics have made it even more so. As a result, superintendents have had to further hone their political skills without allowing political interests to get in the way of educating students.

The increasingly political nature of the superintendency is not only being felt by superintendents themselves, but it is also being acknowledged by others in the education field. The Harvard Graduate School of Education and Claremont Graduate University, for example, have formed the Collaborative on Political Leadership in the Superintendency (CPLS),[1] which is "focused on equipping superintendents with the political acumen to make positive change in a complex environment."[2] Professor Jennifer Perry Cheatham, senior lecturer on Education at the Harvard Graduate School of Education and former superintendent of Madison Metropolitan School District, described the impetus behind this collaborative, saying, "Our concern is that without strong political leadership, our collective efforts to address inequality in education will fail."

The CPLS Framework identifies three dimensions of the political environment that superintendents must understand: (1) Macro: politics at the state and federal level; (2) Meso: politics at the local level; and (3) Micro: their own political views. This chapter delves into the first two of these dimensions, focusing on how superintendents had to skillfully manage politics at every level during the pandemic. First, however, we examine how broader societal issues, specifically around race, ignited a level of unrest across the country that likely heightened people's emotional responses to the challenges wrought by COVID-19.

RISING TENSIONS:
"We are in a dual pandemic."

Emotions ran high during the pandemic and, by all accounts, fueled many of the personal and professional attacks that leaders at all levels endured. Many superintendents, however, cited the murder of George Floyd on May 25, 2020, as the incident that ignited not only widespread public turmoil but also much of the heated backlash they received in the months following.[3] Dr. Matt Miller, former superintendent of Lakota Local Schools in Ohio, Dr. Baron R. Davis, former superintendent of Richland School District Two in South Carolina, and Dr. Joe Gothard, superintendent of Madison Metropolitan School District in Wisconsin, all agreed that the murder of George Floyd marked a shift in how their communities responded to them. Miller talked about the criticism he faced from some community members when he spoke out publicly against Floyd's murder.

While many superintendents felt compelled to address issues of racial and social justice, some, like Dr. Gregory Hutchings, former superintendent in Alexandria City Public Schools in Virginia, were unapologetically outspoken. Hutchings was one of the first to coin the term "dual pandemic," referring to what he and many others identified as the concurrent pandemics of COVID-19 and racism. He vividly remembered what the murder of George Floyd meant to him and how he addressed it head-on in his community:

> I'm not glad about the pandemic, but I'm glad we had people's attention. I think if there [hadn't been] a pandemic we would not have seen the same reaction to George Floyd's murder . . . I think people were able to pay attention to what happened to him, and how it was so unjust.

He went on to say, "Yes, we have COVID but we also have [long-standing] racial inequities that are just being exacerbated, but they were always here." While some lashed out at Hutchings for comparing the pandemic to racism, he stood firm and responded by saying, "Racism is killing people, too."

Not all superintendents were in a position to take as public and controversial a stand as some of these superintendents did, but those who did stood by it. Regardless of their local political context, however, the fact remains that broader societal issues set a backdrop for the pandemic that every school leader had to confront in some way.

CONFLICTING STATE AND FEDERAL GUIDANCE:
"We were often the ones that had to make the call."

Dr. Greg Baker, superintendent of Bellingham Public Schools in Washington state, recalled the moment when he had to decide whether to close schools. He had to manage the tension between waiting for state guidance and making the decision that he knew was right for his community:

> Thursday night, I made the decision—if the state doesn't act, I will. By Friday morning, the governor made the announcement, and we were able to align our messaging with the state's directive. But it was not an easy position to be in by any means.

One of the most significant challenges superintendents faced during the pandemic was the conflicting guidance coming from different levels of government. The federal response, particularly under the Trump administration, was marked by inconsistent messaging and political interference in public health recommendations. The tension between public health experts, such as Dr. Anthony Fauci, and state public health officials created confusion and uncertainty at the local level. As Baker said, "We had to balance conflicting information. At the federal level, we watched a complete mess unfold. At the state level, we had a governor who was trying his best, but even then, the guidance was constantly changing."

Superintendents frequently found themselves caught between adhering to public health guidance and responding to political pressures—both externally and from their own school boards. The polarization of the pandemic, particularly around issues of mask mandates and school closures, further complicated their decision-making processes. In many cases, superintendents had to interpret and implement federal guidelines while also managing the expectations of their local communities, which were often divided along political lines. In some states, the governor's office took the lead in setting pandemic-related policies, including school closures, mask mandates, and reopening plans. However, these state-level directives were not always aligned with what local communities wanted. This lack of alignment put superintendents in the position of being human wishbones, having to navigate the delicate balance between following state orders and addressing local concerns.

This intersection of politics and public health was a significant source of stress for many superintendents. Baker spoke of superintendents' need to become de facto health experts while also managing the educational needs of their districts.

> We moved from being instructional leaders to being health officials. All of a sudden, we felt like we had to be experts in public health, reading all of the guidance and trying to figure out what it meant for our schools. And we did this knowing that our community was looking to us for information—information we could not control. As a result, we bore the brunt of their frustration.

In some instances, superintendents found themselves very publicly at odds with their elected officials. Dr. LaTonya Goffney in Aldine, Texas, along with other superintendents in her state, sued their governor over requiring masks—the state did not want to mandate them, but superintendents felt they had to in order to get teachers and students to return to in-person learning:

> I try not to get into politics, however, it was one of those situations in which I was fighting for our district and fighting to educate kids. The only way our teachers would feel safe was if we required masks. Our parents wanted it, our teachers wanted it. . . . It wasn't political for me. I was doing what was best to be able to educate our kids and keep everybody safe.

Goffney and her fellow superintendents prevailed and moved forward with a mask mandate that gave their staff and students the sense of safety they needed to return to their school buildings. This, however, remains an example of just how political the job became for some superintendents during the pandemic.

Although many felt they were not adequately equipped or trained to manage a public health emergency of this magnitude, superintendents found themselves having to make decisions that would impact the health and safety of thousands. The lack of clear and consistent guidance from health authorities at the state and federal levels, along with pressure from their local communities, made this challenge even harder.

MANAGING LOCAL POLITICS:
"There were times when each day felt like a battle."

As the reality of the pandemic set in, Oakland Unified School District superintendent Kyla Johnson-Trammell faced the daunting task of navigating the highly politicized environment in Oakland, California, a city already known for its complex political dynamics. As she described it, "Oakland is as political a place as you will find anywhere [and] during the pandemic, it was like politics on steroids."

One of the most politically charged decisions Johnson-Trammell had to make was whether to close schools and shift to remote learning. With no clear guidance from state or local authorities and growing concerns in her community, she found herself in a position where she had to take the lead. She said, "I quickly saw that if I waited for guidance, we'd be behind, [so] I told my team, 'We have to do this ourselves.'" This decision to act independently was not without its risks. Johnson-Trammell knew that any misstep could have severe repercussions, both politically and for the students she served. "I had to communicate clearly and decisively, even when I wasn't sure what the right decision was. If I waffled or waited, it would erode trust and create even more political issues."

While some state leaders pushed for schools to reopen quickly, citing economic and social reasons, local leaders, including superintendents, had to be more cautious as they listened to their communities, who were pushing them to prioritize health and safety. This divergence of opinion often placed superintendents in the crossfire between state mandates and local opposition. Kristi, former superintendent of the Buckeye Elementary School District in Arizona and past president of AASA, echoed Baker in the difficult decisions superintendents had to make, saying, "You don't want to be the superintendent to open too quickly and somebody dies. . . . It's just way too much to take on."[4]

The lack of clear guidance from state and local authorities left superintendents in a precarious position. Local politics, including relationships with teachers' unions and school boards, added another layer of complexity to the decision-making process during the pandemic.

Superintendents had to navigate the expectations of parents, staff, and other stakeholders, many of whom had strong opinions on issues such as remote learning, safety protocols, and vaccine mandates.

BALANCING UNION AND SCHOOL BOARD RELATIONSHIPS:
"It was a delicate dance."

The sudden shift to remote learning created an environment of uncertainty and anxiety for everyone involved. Teachers' unions, concerned about the safety and well-being of their members, were quick to seek assurances from school districts. Superintendents found themselves at the forefront of this crisis, needing to provide clear and decisive leadership while also maintaining open lines of communication with union representatives.

Effective superintendents approached this challenge by involving union representatives in the decision-making process. Many districts formed joint committees with union leadership to develop and review safety protocols, including mask mandates, social distancing guidelines, ventilation improvements, and access to personal protective equipment (PPE). By giving unions a seat at the table, superintendents not only improved the quality of the safety measures but also ensured greater buy-in from teachers. Superintendents implemented various strategies to support their teachers' well-being, often in collaboration with unions.

In the initial phase of the pandemic, superintendents who prioritized transparency and collaboration were more successful in managing relationships with their teachers' unions. Frequent virtual meetings, updates, and consultations with union leaders helped to build trust and foster a sense of shared purpose. Superintendents who acknowledged the unions' concerns—ranging from health and safety protocols to job security—were able to create a foundation for cooperation rather than confrontation. Dr. Candy Singh, former superintendent in Fallbrook Union School District in California, cited the strength of her partnership with her teachers' union as one of the most significant contributing factors to their ability to be one of the first districts in California to reopen:

> Because the culture of care in our district was so deep already, we got agreements with our unions in a day. My team and I walked through classrooms with union leaders and asked, "What will make you feel good to get teachers back in here?" And if they said they wanted more plexiglass barriers, then we got more plexiglass barriers. Whatever they said they needed, we did.

This collaborative approach was not universal, however. In some districts, the relationship between superintendents and unions became adversarial, particularly when decisions were made unilaterally or when unions felt their concerns were being dismissed. These tensions often led to public disputes, with unions threatening to do strikes or other forms of protest. This conflict was particularly challenging in districts where the unions had considerable influence. For example, as referenced earlier, Enfield faced tremendous resistance in bringing teachers back to the classroom in Highline Public Schools:

> I reluctantly had to file an injunction against my Pre–K and kindergarten teachers to get them to come back to school for in-person instruction. I truly empathized with them, but at the same time we had surveyed our families and over 45 percent said they wanted their children back in school for at least part of the day or week. It was a mandate I could not ignore.

This situation in Highline was hardly unique—districts across the country found themselves in similar circumstances. Local political dynamics required superintendents to be skilled negotiators, balancing the demands of different groups while maintaining their focus on educational outcomes for students.

Just as they did with their unions, superintendents had to be diligent in ensuring that their school boards were informed at all times on what decisions needed to be made. While always important, strong board relationships were imperative for superintendents during the pandemic, and those who had a strong foundation to build upon were better positioned to lead. In Oakland, for example, where Johnson-Trammell had served as superintendent since 2017, her board knew her and trusted her judgment, which allowed her to act decisively. Her ability to articulate the rationale behind her actions helped reinforce trust and credibility, both with her board and the broader community:

> The one thing I started to see was that everybody thought they were a researcher and a doctor, so I told my team, "We have to look like we know our stuff. When I'm speaking, I have to be able to back [my decisions] with data and research."

Johnson-Trammell's disciplined approach to providing the rationale behind her decisions strengthened trust with her board and community. She also admitted, "There were times when I was pushing so hard to get us back [in school] that I wondered if I was eroding my capital with board members or severing relationships with the teachers union." She remained steadfast in her conviction, however, that getting students back into the classroom was the right thing to do. "It was a moral conviction. I knew it was what needed to happen, even if it was politically risky."

In some districts, superintendents clashed with board members over how to align with state and federal mandates and at the same time respond to the priorities of their staff and families. Board meetings became battlegrounds at times, with superintendents having to brave the demands of angry citizens along with frustrated board members. Even for those who remained in their roles throughout the pandemic, the damage was done, and some found themselves leaving their districts soon after.

ADVOCATING FOR STUDENTS:
"The district became a target because I was willing to stand up for kids."

Throughout the pandemic, superintendents increasingly found themselves in the public eye, often becoming the face of the district's response to

COVID-19. This visibility brought both opportunities and challenges. On the one hand, it allowed superintendents to advocate for their districts at the state and national levels, pushing for necessary resources and support. On the other hand, it exposed them to public scrutiny and criticism, particularly in politically charged environments.

This public role did, however, give superintendents the opportunity to engage in advocacy efforts, both for their districts and for the broader community. Many became vocal advocates for additional funding, mental health resources, and expanded technology access, recognizing that the pandemic was making the existing inequities in education impossible to ignore. Their efforts helped shape state and federal policies, but they also faced resistance from those who viewed their actions as overly cautious or politically motivated. One such effort, organized by a group of superintendents who were all part of the Digital Promise League of Innovative Schools,[5] centered on highlighting the need for universal internet access. They came together and created a social media campaign called "Connect Kids Now," urging elected officials and policymakers to take the necessary steps to ensure that all households had access to reliable internet. Clearly, the campaign did not achieve its goal of establishing universal internet access, but the signal it sent to these superintendents' communities—that they cared about them and were fighting for what they needed—was powerful.

There were also times when superintendents truly risked their careers to advocate for what they believed was right. In South Carolina, Davis made the courageous decision to sue his state over mask mandates. In his words,

> I knew how far I was willing to go to advocate for kids. When it came to the state threatening to defund public education if we required a mask mandate, I sued saying that was unconstitutional. We prevailed but I believe we were retaliated against as a result.

The pandemic thrust superintendents into being vocal advocates. It also accentuated the critical importance of maintaining strong relationships and being astute political leaders. In the face of unprecedented challenges, leaders like Johnson-Trammell, Goffney, and Davis demonstrated remarkable resilience, adaptability, and courage. Their actions not only kept students safe but also ensured that education continued in the most trying of circumstances. Through it all, they remained steadfast advocates for their students, navigating the treacherous waters of politics and public health with grace and determination. Unfortunately, some paid a heavy price.

THE PERSONAL TOLL AND ENDURING CONSEQUENCES:
"Some of us stayed around long enough to become the villains."

The fact that several of the superintendents in this book are no longer in the role is evidence that the political battles of the pandemic took a profound toll. Leaders like Johnson-Trammell and Davis spoke for many of their colleagues when sharing the impact it had on them both personally and professionally. Dr. Kristine Gilmore, former superintendent in D.C. Everest Area School District, however, summed it up poignantly in describing her decision to leave the superintendency after seventeen years: "It [the pandemic] wasn't the only factor, but it certainly was a factor in my decision to go when I did. I loved being a superintendent, but it just wasn't good for me anymore." There clearly remain lingering effects of the pandemic on superintendent turnover.

Analysis from ILO Group's Superintendent Research Project in 2022 revealed that nearly half of the nation's largest school districts have experienced leadership turnover:

> Drawing from The National Center for Education Statistics, we identified the 500 most populous school districts in the country, as well as the superintendent in each district. Since the start of the pandemic in March 2020, 246 (49%) of the 500 most populous school districts in the country have undergone or are currently undergoing leadership changes.[6]

The Superintendent Lab, a center "for data, research, insights, and innovation on the school district superintendency," has also tracked the rate at which superintendents are leaving their jobs. According to Dr. Rachel White, founder of the Lab and an assistant professor of educational leadership and policy studies at the University of Tennessee-Knoxville, superintendent turnover rates increased from 14.2 percent between 2019–2020 and 2020–2021 to 17.1 percent between 2021–22 and 2022–2023.[7]

The impact of this turnover on a district's students, staff, and families can be significant. When a superintendent leaves, the reset button often gets hit on much of the work they were leading, which results in district staff having to stop what they have been doing and start something new. This not only creates chaos; it can also prevent districts from seeing results since it means a particular initiative or strategy may not have sufficient time to show that it is successfully improving student outcomes. Turnover does not only affect the work; it also has a real impact on superintendents themselves.

Dr. Aaron Spence, superintendent in Loudoun County Public Schools in Virginia, a veteran leader who has weathered many political battles, described his experience during the pandemic:

> I stood there in the firing line because I believed in the work we were doing for kids and for families. And people have forgotten that. I think the level of disrespect and incivility, and the discourse about superintendents and about school boards that we're seeing, frankly, is shocking. And it's alarming, because what I think the public probably doesn't fully understand is the degree to which people are giving up on the job.

What came through loud and clear from many of the superintendents interviewed was their love for the work of educating children. It is a love that never wavered, but there came a point when their own mental and physical health suffered, and they had to make the difficult decision to leave. As one former superintendent put it, "We stepped up at times, to our own detriment."

There is definitely a mix of sadness, concern, and hope in the way superintendents reflect on the current state of the profession. Davis expressed this mixture of emotions:

> We need to reaffirm public education, and [educators] and superintendents need to be supported and reaffirmed for what they do. . . . We need to have that spirit again of taking care of each other and having each other's backs. I think that would go a long way, but I don't know how or when that's going to happen.

His point was echoed by Spence:

> It's so brutal out here right now. Maybe this is the thing people in our country need to know: Google the superintendent in your community and see the horrible, nasty things people say about them. And then try to remember that these are people who get up every morning and go to work to make a difference in your child's life.

In spite of it all, these leaders would do it all again, as Miller conveyed when reflecting on his experience as a superintendent leading during the pandemic:

> If you had told me that at the beginning [of the pandemic] that all these bad things could happen to your kids and to your community, but you're going to get everybody through all that, but it might cost you your job, would you do it? I would.

Superintendents know that being a leader in the public eye brings scrutiny, criticism, and sometimes attacks. During the pandemic, however, those attacks escalated, leading to an increase in superintendents leaving their jobs. Those who remain in the role, along with those who have left, however, stand firm in putting students ahead of politics—even though they know there is often a price to pay.

EXEMPLARY LEADERSHIP: DR. JOE GOTHARD, SUPERINTENDENT OF MADISON PUBLIC SCHOOLS, WISCONSIN, FORMER SUPERINTENDENT OF ST. PAUL PUBLIC SCHOOLS, MINNESOTA

St. Paul Public Schools (SPPS), the second-largest school district in Minnesota, is a diverse system serving 33,000 students across 68 schools. More than 115 languages are spoken by students, and the district's mission is "both bold and simple: to inspire students to think critically, pursue their dreams and change the world." In 2018, then-superintendent Gothard led the development of the district's strategic plan, "SPPS Achieves." The plan focused on these strategic priorities: to create a system of culturally responsive instruction, engage with St. Paul families, and improve the literacy and math proficiency rates for historically underserved students.

For Gothard, the onset of the pandemic was compounded by local crises that would have tested even the most seasoned leader. As the world grappled with an emerging global health crisis, he was navigating not only the complexities of distance learning but also the emotional and political fallout from a teachers' strike and the tragic death of his board chair.

In early March 2020, SPPS was embroiled in intense contract negotiations with the teachers' union. The situation was dire: the district and union were tens of millions of dollars apart from reaching an agreement. As tensions escalated, the union called for a strike—the first in SPPS since 1946. At the same time, news of a mysterious virus spreading overseas was beginning to make its way to the United States. "Talk of the Coronavirus—at the time we didn't call it COVID yet—was all over from overseas," Gothard noted, signaling the impending crisis that would soon overshadow the strike.

Amid the strike, the district faced a stark reality. Teachers were demonstrating in the streets, and the union showed no signs of budging. The national spotlight was on SPPS, with prominent national leaders like Randy Weingarten, president of the American Federation of Teachers, joining the fray. The situation reached a critical point when the governor intervened, calling Gothard and a small team to a mediation session:

He talked to both us and the union together in a small group and told us that he had no idea what was about to happen, but the talks of this [virus] being called a pandemic were real, and we had to get this contract settled,

Gothard recalled. With the threat of a pandemic looming, the strike ended after twenty-four hours of nonstop bargaining.

Gothard and his team had little time to rest, much less celebrate, as they were immediately confronted with the task of transitioning to remote learning. The decision to keep students out of school for the first week was a pragmatic one, as it allowed the district time to prepare for an unprecedented shift in how education would be delivered. "We had three weeks to plan. We had spring break right in the middle," he explained, highlighting the logistical complexities of the situation. The district moved quickly, deploying devices to students, securing hotspots for those without internet access, and setting up systems to deliver meals.

Yet, the challenges extended beyond logistics. Negotiating a Memorandum of Understanding with their teachers' union around remote learning expectations proved to be one of the most significant hurdles. "We faced opposition in asking our teachers to do synchronous learning. Our union leadership did not want our teachers to have to be on camera," Gothard said. While he understood their concerns, he knew he had to balance them with what he believed was in the best interest of students. This balancing act would become an ongoing challenge as he and other superintendents worked to keep student well-being front and center—but not at the expense of their staff.

Gothard's challenges were not limited to teaching and learning, however. In May 2020, tragedy struck when his board chair, Marny Xiong, succumbed to COVID-19. Xiong, just thirty-one years old, had been a close colleague, and her death was a personal and professional blow to Gothard and the district (see figure 7.1). "She was so young. She and her father were both admitted to the hospital with COVID. They were both placed on ventilators. Her elderly father made it out, but I never again talked to Marny," he recounted. This tragedy was compounded by the murder of George Floyd, which occurred just 9 miles from Gothard's home, igniting protests and riots across Minneapolis-St. Paul and the country. "It wasn't just school, it was everything else that was coming into the space from politics to the history of civil rights in our country," he said.

In the face of these overwhelming political challenges, Gothard remained committed to supporting his staff and students. He quickly recognized the importance of building a strong, supportive community within the district. "I learned really quickly that this wasn't a solo act in terms of leadership. It really had to be distributed, and not just symbolically. It had to be distributed

Figure 7.1. Superintendent Joe Gothard and Marny Xiong at a community event celebrating her election to the SPPS Board of Education in 2017. *Source*: Photograph courtesy of Joe Gothard.

because I didn't know how to do certain things," he explained. Gothard initiated regular virtual meetings, town halls, and Q&A sessions to keep everyone connected and informed. "What I could do is support people. I could thank people. I could allow for safe places for people to have disagreements, even publicly," he added, emphasizing the importance of fostering open communication and mutual support during such a difficult time.

Rather than focusing solely on challenges, Gothard also saw the opportunity to transform SPPS using the federal ESSER funds. When he learned that the district would receive $207 million from the third round of the American Rescue Plan (ARP), Gothard knew this infusion of funds was a once-in-a-lifetime opportunity to innovate. "I thought to myself, $207 million, there's no way I will only spend this money doing what we've done. This is a chance that I'll never have in my career again," he recalled. Under his leadership, the district launched the Office of Innovation and introduced new initiatives, including a focus on the science of reading, partnerships with community organizations, and the creation of new schools like the East African Elementary Magnet School.

Gothard's commitment to innovation was matched by his dedication to maintaining strong relationships within the district and with external partners. "Our way of survival as superintendents was really our networks and connecting to others," he reflects. This collaborative approach, which included close coordination with city and county leaders, was critical to his political leadership in navigating the complexities of the pandemic. "Why did we have to wait for things to be hard to come together and collaborate that way? What would happen if we collaborated like that when things are great?"

In reflecting on his leadership during the pandemic, Gothard emphasized the importance of humility, patience, and authenticity. The challenges he faced required him to be open about what he didn't know and to rely on the collective strength of his team. "I had to be really comfortable kind of being the opposite of that—being vulnerable. And I do think people appreciated it," he said. This openness, coupled with a deep sense of empathy for his staff and students, helped Gothard lead his district through one of the most challenging periods in its history. His story is a testament to the resilience, creativity, and dedication required to manage the politics of leading a school district through multiple crises at once.

INSIGHTS AND TAKEAWAYS FROM MANAGING POLITICS

- *Superintendents are political leaders*. Superintendents must be true to their own values, but at the same time their personal politics come second to doing what is best for their districts. While not easy, it is necessary if they are to build the trust and credibility to remain in their roles long enough to enact meaningful, lasting change for students.
- *Students before politics*. Every decision a superintendent makes will be criticized by someone. This is why having a strong and clear conviction about keeping the best interests of students at the center of their decisions is essential. Developing a thick skin, along with building a coalition of support within the community, helps make the criticism manageable.
- *School board elections matter*. Relationships with school boards can make or break a superintendent, and turnover on a school board can erode the stability of a district for good and bad. In an increasingly polarized national context, voters must seek out candidates committed to putting students, not agendas, first.

The hard-won lessons of the pandemic will continue to shape the way that superintendents, boards of education, and teachers' unions work together to serve and support children and families. Superintendents played a critical role in navigating the political complexities, and their ability to balance conflicting guidance, manage local political dynamics, and advocate for their districts was essential to the continued functioning of the education system during this unprecedented crisis—and for some, it cost them their jobs. Moving forward, the lessons learned from this period will be invaluable in shaping the future of educational leadership, ensuring that our school system and its leaders are better prepared to face the inevitable challenges to come.

NOTES

1. Collaborative on Political Leadership in the Superintendency (CPLS), https://cpl-s.com.

2. Harvard Graduate School of Education and Claremont Graduate University, "Political Leadership in the Superintendency," February 2024, 1–9, https://cpl-s.com/wp-content/uploads/2024/03/Emergent-Framework-REVISED-Feb-2024.pdf.

3. "How the Murder of George Floyd Changed K–12 Schooling: A Collection," *Education Week,* https://www.edweek.org/leadership/how-the-murder-of-george-floyd-changed-k-12-schooling-a-collection.

4. Nicole Gaudiano and Dan Goldberg, "'It's Just Way Too Much to Take On': School Systems Struggle with the Politics of Reopening," *Politico,* May 17, 2020, https://www.politico.com/news/2020/06/17/reopening-schools-coronavirus-327020.

5. Digital Promise, League of Innovative Schools, https://digitalpromise.org/initiative/league-of-innovative-schools/.

6. ILO Group, "Updated Analysis Shows Leadership Disruption Impacts Almost Half of Nation's Largest School Districts," December 12, 2022, https://www.ilogroup.com/wp-content/uploads/2022/12/The-Superintendent-Research-Project_Dec-2022-Update.pdf.

7. Evie Blad, "High Pace of Superintendent Turnover Continues, Data Show," *Education Week,* September 19, 2023, https://www.edweek.org/leadership/high-pace-of-superintendent-turnover-continues-data-show/2023/09; Superintendent Lab, https://thesuperintendentlab.com/.

Chapter 8

Threats and Opportunities Moving Forward

> It's a noble profession, we are in it to improve society, but if we don't start paying close attention to what's happening, we are in trouble.
>
> — Melvin Brown, Superintendent of Montgomery Public Schools, Alabama

Public education has long been a battleground for differing opinions. Critics argue for reforms that make schools more fair, responsive, and accessible, while some evangelical Christians, cultural conservatives, and corporate capitalists push for changes that align with their specific ideologies or financial interests. On the other hand, supporters see public education as largely succeeding in its mission to help all students develop knowledge, skills, and civic responsibility. This ongoing debate, fueled by both supporters and critics, has the potential to either erode or strengthen public education.

This final chapter delves into the key threats and opportunities facing superintendents in the post-pandemic era, including the impact of national politics, the rise of school choice, shifting school board dynamics, the rapid development of artificial intelligence (AI), and the necessity for public schools to protect themselves from becoming obsolete. Superintendents will be instrumental in shaping the future of public education, finding new and innovative ways to provide all students with the personalized, high-quality education they deserve. They cannot, however, do this without the support of their school boards and communities.

POLARIZATION AND PARTISANSHIP:
"We have to find ways to bring people along."

The political climate at the federal, state, and local levels grew more polarized during the pandemic, seeping into school districts and turning issues like mask mandates, vaccine requirements, curriculum content, and social justice initiatives into flashpoints at school board meetings. For some districts, this polarization began long before COVID-19, while for others, it was the pandemic that ignited it in their communities. Regardless, districts continue to grapple with an increasingly challenging political environment.

Once seen as neutral educational leaders, superintendents now find themselves at the center of these political battles. This polarization has challenged their ability to lead effectively, as any decision can provoke fierce opposition from one side of the political spectrum or the other. Matt Miller, former superintendent of Lakota Local School District in Ohio, firmly believes that the groundwork for this shift began before the onset of the pandemic:

> The national movement of fringe groups against superintendents as leaders didn't start with COVID-19. It started with George Floyd's murder. When that happened I, like, many of my colleagues, put out communications condemning his murder and publicly supporting our students of color. That stirred something in some fringe groups. That was the beginning of superintendents becoming political targets, and then the pandemic spurred even more hate and anger against us.

Despite these challenges, superintendents understand their responsibility to lead with a vision that transcends political divides. By focusing on the shared goal of providing a high-quality education for all students, they can build consensus among diverse stakeholders. Achieving this consensus requires strong communication, transparency, and a commitment to listening to all voices within the community. Those who can successfully navigate these political waters may even emerge as unifying figures, capable of bringing together different groups for the common good.

FEDERAL AND STATE OVERREACH:
"Sometimes it can be difficult to innovate with
so much red tape."

The increased involvement of federal and state governments in local education, often driven by political agendas, has added another layer of complexity to the superintendency. Policies related to standardized testing, school funding, and curriculum standards are frequently influenced by national political trends, requiring superintendents to balance these external pressures while maintaining focus on their district's specific needs. One prominent example has been the push to remove books from school libraries or, in some cases, to ban certain books altogether. In states like Florida, Alabama, and Virginia, among others, elected officials have taken further steps to dictate what schools can and cannot teach.[1]

Amid these potential threats, superintendents are in a unique position to advocate for their districts at the local, state, and federal levels. By building strong relationships with policymakers and staying informed about legislative developments, superintendents can influence education policy in ways that benefit their students, staff, and families. While this advocacy role allows superintendents to be proactive in shaping education rather than merely reacting to external pressures, it is not always easy to balance politics with advocacy.

Dr. Baron Davis, former superintendent in Richland School District Two, described this tension, saying, "Sometimes your job is 80 percent politics and 20 percent advocacy, and sometimes it's reversed. I do know that they go hand in hand, and finding the right balance is critical, but I can't see one existing without the other." Davis walked his talk in this respect when, as discussed earlier, he sued the governor and the State of South Carolina over the attempt to withhold state funding to school districts that mandated that students wear masks once they returned to school in person. School superintendents can and must continue to be advocates for students while also being aware of the political costs of doing so, costs that can include making themselves or their districts targets for retaliation.

EXPANSION OF SCHOOL CHOICE AND VOUCHERS:
"The voucher movement will drain state budgets with little accountability of the use of funds."

The post-pandemic period has seen a surge in support for school choice with charter schools and voucher programs, along with homeschooling, gaining momentum across the country. Proponents argue that these options provide families with greater flexibility and can spur innovation in education. However, the expansion of school choice presents a significant threat to traditional public school districts, particularly in terms of funding and enrollment. Superintendents must contend with the financial implications of losing enrollment because of the school choice movement that includes charter schools and private institutions.

The school choice movement has been steadily growing among marginalized groups like evangelical Christians (who resist public schools because of disagreements over secular humanism, LGBTQ rights, views of God among other issues), cultural conservatives (who resist public schools because of disagreements over the exposure to antiracism and other tenets of liberalism), corporate capitalists (who resist teachers' unions), and libertarians (who resist compulsory education as one of the most significant government interventions in private life). Billionaires and millionaires have also been part of the school choice movement, seeing public schools and K–12 education as another sector with the potential for disruption, including for-profit alternatives.[2] The purpose of uniting these various groups is essentially to dismantle public education. The movement is growing from state to state, negatively impacting school funding and leading to the expansion of voucher programs. These voucher programs or policies allow families to take a portion of their state's education funding away from public schools to pay for their child's private education. Those who support voucher programs believe that universal expansion would be a better use of public funds, with some framing public schools as "government schools" or merely welfare programs.

While the rise of school choice challenges public schools, it also presents an opportunity for innovation. Superintendents can seize this chance to rethink traditional models of education and explore new approaches to teaching and learning. By embracing innovation, investing in teachers, and creating more personalized and engaging learning environments, public schools can position themselves as competitive options for families. Superintendents are well positioned to take the initiative, lead transformational change, and demonstrate the unique value of public education.

School choice also raises concerns about equity. While some families may benefit from greater educational options, others—particularly those in underserved communities—may find themselves left behind. Superintendents must address the potential for increased segregation and disparities in educational quality as a result of school choice policies. They must be champions for educational equity in the face of school choice. By advocating for policies that ensure all students, regardless of background or socioeconomic status, have access to high-quality education, superintendents can work to close achievement gaps and promote inclusivity. This work may involve developing programs that specifically target underserved populations or creating partnerships with community organizations to provide additional support for students.

Superintendents will also have to focus their attention on national policies around the school choice movement, as these policies could directly impact funding and potentially undermine the foundation of public education. What started with divisiveness and disdain for superintendent leadership during COVID-19 has led to an expansion of homeschooling and voucher programs.

With more public funding across states going to private entities, Dr. Melvin Brown, superintendent of Montgomery Public Schools in Alabama, expressed serious concern, saying, "The people who want to erode public education will not stop." In his view, the expansion of public funding will go beyond public education and reach into privatizing other organizations, with the ultimate goal being to privatize the broader public sector.

THE EVOLVING ROLE OF SCHOOL BOARDS:
"School board races now matter more than ever."

School boards, which have traditionally served as governance bodies focused on policy and oversight, have become increasingly activist and partisan in the post-pandemic era. The heightened visibility of education issues, driven by media coverage and social media, has led to more contentious board meetings and greater scrutiny of superintendents' decisions. Miller summarized this particular challenge from his experiences in Ohio:

> I had two people [running for the board who were] backed by fringe groups. Voter turnout was so low, maybe 16 percent, and they were backed by people that had money. Their values and mission did not align with public education at all, and they did not support the work of the district, but they had the financial backing to win in this political climate.

This increased activism of school boards, however, does present an opportunity for superintendents to strengthen governance practices within their districts. By fostering a collaborative and transparent relationship with board members, superintendents can ensure that decision-making is informed by data, best practices, and the needs of the community. The more effectively superintendents engage with the public, the more they help to build trust and support for their district's work.

The relationship between the superintendent and the school board is critical to the success of any district initiative and to the longevity of the superintendent. In the post-pandemic world, where boards are more polarized and consequently more engaged, this relationship has become more complex. A breakdown in this relationship can lead to instability and turnover in district leadership, which ultimately harms students and staff. At the same time, the issue of board turnover is equally real, as Davis described:

> [Some] good board members just got worn out and didn't run and that opened the door for very conservative Moms for Liberty candidates with very partisan agendas. My board flipped, so I decided it was time to part ways.

Superintendents can view the changing dynamics of school boards as a way to build stronger, more productive relationships with board members and the broader community. Prioritizing regular communication, setting clear expectations, and working collaboratively to align goals are important, but so is helping communities understand the impact of board elections on their schools and their superintendents.

THE ADVENT OF AI:
"AI has the power to change the world but nothing will ever replace teachers."

AI is rapidly transforming various sectors, and education is no exception. While AI offers opportunities to enhance educational outcomes, it also presents significant ethical concerns, particularly regarding data privacy, bias in algorithms, and the potential for AI to replace the work of humans. Additionally, the rise of AI could lead to shifts in the roles and responsibilities of teachers and administrators, raising concerns about job security and the devaluation of human expertise.

How superintendents present their knowledge and application of generative AI (GenAI) tools will directly impact the path forward. GenAI, powered by models like OpenAI's ChatGPT, Google's Bard, and others, has the potential to revolutionize the way we teach and the way that students learn.[3]

As AI gains a greater foothold in our world, some wonder if the use of AI tools will make teachers unnecessary. The answer is clear: AI cannot and will not replace teachers in the classroom. The need for human connection remains a constant and primary factor for student achievement to occur, just as was realized during the pandemic. While AI can be a powerful tool, teachers will remain essential in educating students and supporting them in dealing with the stress of learning difficult material and also the trauma that many students experience and carry with them to school.[4]

Superintendents do face the dilemma of finding and presenting balanced approaches to incorporating AI into current curriculum policies. It can be challenging, for example, to ensure that a curriculum focuses sufficiently on literacy, mathematics, and science—and that it helps students think critically, solve problems collaboratively, and use AI tools to find answers to complex problems.

AI presents an exciting opportunity for superintendents to lead the integration of cutting-edge technology in education. By adopting AI tools thoughtfully and ethically, superintendents can enhance personalized learning, streamline administrative processes, and provide teachers with valuable insights to support student achievement. Moreover, AI can help districts become more efficient, allowing resources to be allocated more effectively. Superintendents can lead the charge in ensuring that AI is used to complement, rather than replace, the human elements of teaching and learning.

At the same time, the rapid pace of technological change poses a significant challenge for school districts, particularly those with limited resources. Keeping up with the latest AI developments, ensuring equitable access to technology, and preparing staff to use these tools effectively are all daunting tasks for superintendents. Those who embrace AI and other emerging technologies, however, can position their districts as leaders in educational innovation. By investing in professional development, fostering a culture of experimentation, and engaging with technology partners, superintendents can drive the adoption of new tools that enhance teaching and learning.

THE THREAT OF BECOMING OBSOLETE:
"If we don't change, kids and teachers will vote with their feet."

The real risk of obsolescence comes from within the education system itself. If we continue to do things the way we always have, we risk failing to give students what they need to succeed in a rapidly changing world. Superintendents must recognize that the traditional model of education is under threat, not only from external factors but also from within. If we fail to adapt and innovate, we risk becoming obsolete. During COVID-19, the education system demonstrated that it could function differently, but most would argue that the system has largely reverted to pre-pandemic practices. Some districts, especially those led by forward-thinking boards and superintendents, however, are committed to using lessons from the pandemic to transform how we teach and learn.

This is about more than innovation; it is about survival, according to Dr. Aaron Spence, superintendent of Loudoun County Public Schools in Virginia. He believes that if we don't fundamentally change our school systems, then teachers, students, and parents may eventually abandon public education altogether. Seeing this as a looming threat, Spence and his leadership team and board are working to be responsive to the changing needs of teachers and students.

> During COVID we demonstrated that you could still run school and have Mondays without students for teachers to plan, [but then] we went back to the traditional five-day week. So this year we've added sixteen more days into the calendar for teacher planning. Maybe [moving forward] we extend that deeper into the school year and return to giving teachers Mondays for planning

purposes only, not instruction. Fortunately, I have a board that is interested in having that conversation, which I'm grateful for. I don't know what will come of it, but [as I said] if we don't do something, teachers will vote with their feet, kids will vote with their feet, parents will vote with their feet, and then we truly will become obsolete.

Spence's assessment is a call to action for superintendents to serve as their districts' lead innovators. There are very real challenges and threats, but at the same time, superintendents and others committed to service in public education can collectively choose to move our education system forward in new and exciting ways.

The post-pandemic era presents a complex landscape for school superintendents, characterized by significant threats and promising opportunities. National politics, the rise of school choice, the changing dynamics of school boards, and the advent of AI, all pose challenges that require careful navigation and strategic leadership. Within these challenges, however, lie opportunities for superintendents to lead transformational change and advocate for the well-being of their students and communities. By embracing these opportunities while also addressing the associated threats with creativity, vision, courage, and collaboration, superintendents can not only weather the challenges of the post-pandemic era but also drive much-needed improvements in our public schools.

FINAL REFLECTIONS

In the course of interviewing superintendents for this book, what was most stunning, though not surprising, was the consistency in themes that emerged. First, these leaders are not in this work for the money or title. They choose to be superintendents because they truly care about making a difference in the lives of children and the communities they serve. Second, they want to be seen first and foremost as people. As the political nature of the superintendency has become more complex in recent years, superintendents have increasingly become political targets. As a result, there is now a tremendous need to humanize superintendents so that they can garner the support they need from their school boards and communities to remain in their roles and lead our schools long enough to enact lasting, meaningful change.

On Fire

The stories here make it abundantly clear that superintendents stepped up in incredible ways during the pandemic. All whom we spoke to agreed that they worked harder in the first few months of 2020 than they ever had before. While hard work is nothing new to superintendents, it was the magnitude of the moment that made this time so incredibly challenging. Nonetheless, each said the work was intensely gratifying. Having to quickly become public health experts and respond to problems that were entirely unfamiliar—all while ensuring students, staff, and families were safe and supported—pushed them but did not break them. Superintendents truly were "on fire" during this time, performing heroic work on a daily basis.

Under Fire

Superintendents are all too familiar with criticism and even professional and personal attacks. Sadly, that is simply part of being a leader in our highly politicized environment. During the pandemic, however, people hurled their anger, fear, and frustration at superintendents in inappropriate ways. Among other things, some accused superintendents of not caring whether children lived or died. This particular accusation was not only untrue; it was unfair and painfully felt by superintendents who have devoted their careers to ensuring the education, safety, and well-being of children. In spite of being "under fire," however, superintendents remained strong and focused on doing what needed to be done.

Fired

Many of those interviewed for this book are no longer sitting superintendents. Some chose to leave their districts, while others were forced out by their school boards. Some of those who left are still serving as superintendents in other districts, but many have left the profession altogether. This trend should concern everyone who cares about our public education system. Strong, successful schools require strong, supported leadership, and the current rate of superintendent turnover has the potential to weaken our public schools.

We hope that the stories and insights offered here will help new and future superintendents understand the very political nature of this role, along with the tremendous opportunity they have to positively impact not just their districts but their communities as well. We also hope that everyone, in and outside of the education system, understands how instrumental superintendents are to our education system.

The superintendency is made up of rare individuals who share a common purpose—to make a difference in the lives of children. We are here for one another, coming into the job, doing the job, and leaving the job. We are here for one another, knowing what is at stake. We now need our communities to be here for us as well.

NOTES

1. USAFacts Team, "Which States Passed Laws Restricting School Curriculum? Seven States Passed Laws to Restrict Discussion of Race, Gender Identity or Sexual Orientation in Public Schools in 2022," *USAFacts*, March 30, 2023, https://usafacts.org/articles/which-states-passed-laws-restricting-school-curriculum/.

2. Anya Kamenetz, 2022. "School Is for Everyone." *New York Times*, September 1, 2022, https://www.nytimes.com/2022/09/01/opinion/us-school-history.html.

3. Mark Quartararo, "The Impact of Generative AI on Education," *ACEDS Blog, Artificial Intelligence, Data and Technology*, October 25, 2023, https://aceds.org/the-impact-of-generative-ai-on-education-aceds-blog/.

4. Sarah D. Sparks, "Why Teacher-Student Relationships Matter," *Education Week*, March 12, 2019, https://www.edweek.org/teaching-learning/why-teacher-student-relationships-matter/2019/03.

Bibliography

AASA. "Early Learning Cohort." August 14, 2024. https://www.aasa.org/professional-learning/event/2024/08/14/default-calendar/early-learning-cohort.

Barger, Michael M., Elizabeth Moorman Kim, Nathan R. Kuncel, and Eva M. Pomerantz. "The Relation between Parents' Involvement in Children's Schooling and Children's Adjustment: A Meta-Analysis." *Psychological Bulletin* 145, no. 9 (2019): 855–90. https://doi.org/10.1037/bul0000201.

Blad, Evie. "High Pace of Superintendent Turnover Continues, Data Show." *Education Week,* September 19, 2023. https://www.edweek.org/leadership/high-pace-of-superintendent-turnover-continues-data-show/2023/09.

Camera, Lauren. "Ohio Governor Mike DeWine Orders All K–12 Schools Closed." *U.S. News and World Report,* March 12, 2020.

Chappell, Bill. "First Known U.S. COVID-19 Death Was Weeks Earlier Than Previously Thought." *National Public Radio,* April 22, 2020. https://www.npr.org/sections/coronavirus-live-updates/2020/04/22/84083618/.

Cheung, Cecilia Sin-Sze, and Eva M. Pomerantz. "Why Does Parents' Involvement Enhance Children's Achievement? The Role of Parent-Oriented Motivation." *Journal of Educational Psychology* 104, no. 3 (2012): 820–32. https://doi.org/10.1037/a0027183.

Chiefs for Change and Council of Chief State School Officers. "Day in the Life of (DILO) Resources." July 2020. https://chiefsforchange.org/wp-content/uploads/2020/08/200801-1000-DILO-simulation-and-resources.pdf.

"Chronic Absence." Attendance Works. https://www.attendanceworks.org/chronic-absence/the-problem.

"Chronic Absenteeism in the Nation's Schools: A Hidden Educational Crisis." U.S. Department of Education, June 2016, updated January 2019. https://www2.ed.gov/datastory/chronicabsenteeism.html.

Collaborative on Political Leadership in the Superintendency (CPLS). https://cpl-s.com.

D'Auria, Gemma, and Aaron De Smet. "Leadership in a Crisis: Responding to the Coronavirus Outbreak and Future Challenges." March 16, 2020. https://www.mckinsey.com/capabilities/people-and-organizational-performance/our-insights/leadership-in-a-crisis-responding-to-the-coronavirus-outbreak-and-future-challenges.

Dearing, Eric, Kathleen McCartney, Heather B. Weiss, Holly Kreider, and Sandra Simpkins. "The Promotive Effects of Family Educational Involvement for Low-Income Children's Literacy." *Journal of School Psychology* 42, no. 6 (2004): 445–60. http://doi.org/10.1016/j.jsp.2004.07.002.

Department of Education, Office of Elementary and Secondary Education. Elementary and Secondary School Emergency Relief Fund. https://oese.ed.gov/offices/education-stabilization-fund/elementary-secondary-school-emergency-relief-fund/.

Digital Promise, League of Innovative Schools. https://digitalpromise.org/initiative/league-of-innovative-schools/.

Enfield, Susan. "Delivering on Equity Post-Pandemic: Will We or Won't We?" *EdSurge,* January 5, 2021. https://www.edsurge.com/news/2021-01-05-delivering-on-equity-post-pandemic-will-we-or-won-t-we.

Fahle, Erin M., Thomas J. Kane, Tyler Patterson, Sean F. Reardon, Douglas O. Staiger, Elizabeth A. Stuart. "School District and Community Factors Associated With Learning Loss During the COVID-19 Pandemic." Center for Education Policy Research at Harvard University and Educational Opportunity Project at Stanford University (May 2023): 1–65. https://cepr.harvard.edu/sites/hwpi.harvard.edu/files/cepr/files/explaining_covid_losses_5.23.pdf.

Fauci, Anthony. *On Call: A Doctor's Journey in Public Service*. New York: Viking, 2024.

Gallup and Learning Heroes. "B-flation: How Good Grades Can Sideline Parents." 2023. https://bealearninghero.org/wp-content/uploads/2023/11/B-flation_Gallup_Learning-Heroes_Report-FINAL.pdf.

Gaudiano, Nicole, and Dan Goldberg. "'It's Just Way Too Much to Take On': School Systems Struggle with the Politics of Reopening." *Politico*, May 17, 2020. https://www.politico.com/news/2020/06/17/reopening-schools-coronavirus-327020.

Golden, Alexandrea R., Emily N. Srisarajivakul, Amanda J. Hasselle, Rory A. Pfund, and Jerica Knox. "What Was a Gap Is Now a Chasm: Remote Schooling, the Digital Divide, and Educational Inequities Resulting from the COVID-19 Pandemic." *Current Opinion in Psychology*, June 12, 2023. https://doi.org/10.1016/j.copsyc.2023.101632.

Grolnick, Wendy S., and Maria L. Slowiaczek. "Parents' Involvement in Children's Schooling: A Multidimensional Conceptualization and Motivational Model." *Child Development* 65, no. 1 (1994): 237–52. https://doi.org/10.2307/1131378.

Haderlein, Shira K., Anna Rosefsky Saavedra, Morgan S. Polikoff, Daniel Silver, Amie Rapaport, and Marshall Garland. "Disparities in Educational Access in the Time of COVID: Evidence from a Nationally Representative Panel of American Families." *American Educational Research Association (AERA) Open* 7 (August 23, 2021). https://doi.org/10.1177/23328584211041350.

Hallett, Vicky. "Does Homework Still Have Value? A Johns Hopkins Education Expert Weighs In." Johns Hopkins University Hub, January 17, 2024. https://hub.jhu.edu/2024/01/17/are-we-assigning-too-much-homework.

Harvard Graduate School of Education and Claremont Graduate University. "Political Leadership in the Superintendency." February 2024, 1–9. https://cpl-s.com/wp-content/uploads/2024/03/Emergent-Framework-REVISED-Feb-2024.pdf.

Hong, Sehee, and Hsiu-Zu Ho. "Direct and Indirect Longitudinal Effects of Parental Involvement on Student Achievement: Second-Order Latent Growth Modeling across Ethnic Groups." *Journal of Educational Psychology* 97, no. 1 (2005): 32–42. https://doi.org/10.1037/0022-0663.97.1.32.

"How the Murder of George Floyd Changed K–12 Schooling: A Collection." *Education Week,* 2020–2021. https://www.edweek.org/leadership/how-the-murder-of-george-floyd-changed-k-12-schooling-a-collection.

ILO Group. "Updated Analysis Shows Leadership Disruption Impacts Almost Half of Nation's Largest School Districts." December 12, 2022. https://www.ilogroup.com/wp-content/uploads/2022/12/The-Superintendent-Research-Project_Dec-2022-Update.pdf.

Kamenetz, Anya. "School Is for Everyone." *New York Times,* September 1, 2022. https://www.nytimes.com/2022/09/01/opinion/us-school-history.html.

Li, Fengxiao. "Impact of COVID-19 on the Lives and Mental Health of Children and Adolescents." *Frontiers in Public Health* 10 (2022). https://doi.org/10.3389/fpubh.2022.925213.

Malkus, Nat. "Long COVID for Public Schools: Chronic Absenteeism before and after the Pandemic." American Enterprise Institute, January 31, 2024. https://www.aei.org/research-products/report/long-covid-for-public-schools-chronic-absenteeism-before-and-after-the-pandemic/.

Peterson, Paul E., David M. Houston, and Martin R. West. "Parental Anxieties over Student Learning Dissipate as Schools Relax Anti-Covid Measures." *Education Next,* Winter 2023. https://www.educationnext.org/wp-content/uploads/2022/12/ednext_XXIII_1_ednext_parent_survey.pdf.

Quartararo, Mark. "The Impact of Generative AI on Education." *ACEDS Blog, Artificial Intelligence, Data and Technology,* October 25, 2023. https://aceds.org/the-impact-of-generative-ai-on-education-aceds-blog/.

Saad, Lydia. "Americans' Satisfaction with K–12 Education on Low Side." Gallup, September 1, 2022. https://news.gallup.com/poll/399731/americans-satisfaction-education-low-side.aspx.

Sparks, Sarah D. "Why Teacher-Student Relationships Matter." *Education Week,* March 12, 2019. https://www.edweek.org/teaching-learning/why-teacher-student-relationships-matter/2019/03.

Spector, Carrie. "New Report Shows Historic Gains in Pandemic Recovery For Many U.S. School Districts," Research Stories, Stanford Graduate School of Education, January 31, 2024. https://ed.stanford.edu/news/new-report-shows-historic-gains-pandemic-recovery-many-us-school-districts.

Stanford, Libby. "What the Parents' Rights Movement Forced Schools to Do." *Education Week*, April 25, 2024. https://www.edweek.org/leadership/what-the-parents-rights-movement-forced-schools-to-do/2024/04.

Superintendent Lab. https://thesuperintendentlab.com/.

"Thirty-three Percent of Fourth-Graders at or above NAEP Proficient in Reading, Lower Compared to 2019." NAEP Report Card: Reading, 2022. https://www.nationsreportcard.gov/reading/nation/achievement/?grade=4.

USAFacts Team. "How Many US Children Receive a Free or Reduced-Price School Lunch?" *USAFacts,* October 26, 2023. https://usafacts.org/articles/how-many-us-children-receive-a-free-or-reduced-price-school-lunch/.

USAFacts Team. "Which States Passed Laws Restricting School Curriculum?" *USAFacts*, March 30, 2023. https://usafacts.org/articles/which-states-passed-laws-restricting-school-curriculum/.

U.S. Department of Agriculture. "USDA Extends Free Meals for Kids through December 31, 2020." August 31, 2020. https://www.usda.gov/media/press-releases/2020/08/31/usda-extends-free-meals-kids-through-december-31-2020.

Weir, Kirsten. "Is Homework a Necessary Evil?" *American Psychological Association* 47, no. 3 (2016): 36. https://www.apa.org/monitor/2016/03/homework.

"What's the Difference between Chronic Absence and Truancy?" Attendance Works, January 11, 2016. https://www.attendanceworks.org/whats-the-difference-between-chronic-absence-and-truancy/.

Index

academic support, 37
Academy for Energy and International Business, 102–3
access to diverse perspectives, 32
advent of AI, 128–29
advocating for students, 113–14
American Association of School Administrators (AASA), 9, 21
American Rescue Plan (ARP), 34, 119
annually engage stakeholders, 48
artificial intelligence (AI), 98, 123, 128–29
Auburn School District (ASD), 10–11

Baker, Greg, 109–10
balancing union and school board relationships: collaborative approach, 112; decision-making process, 112; Highline Public Schools, 112–13; initial phase of pandemic, 112; Johnson-Trammell's disciplined approach, 113; remote learning, 111
Balderas, Gustavo, 78
belt-tightening, 36
Biden, Jill, 75
Brown, Melvin, 21, 127
building: relationships in informal networks, 19–21; resilient and viable systems, 32; trust with families, 89

Cajon Valley Union School District (CVUSD), 79; Assistant Superintendent Minshew, 81–82; blended learning models, 80; childcare, 80; communication, 81; community trust, 81; learning challenges and teacher burnout, 80–81; learning management system, 79–80; mental health and wellness initiatives, 81; priority, 82; shared recognition, 82–83
Career and Technical Education (CTE) programs, 101, 103
Care Team, 56
caring for staff, 56; Building Learning Advocates, 65; certificated staff members, 57–58; children graduate, 64; educational experiences, 64; flexibility, 65; great empathy, 58; isolation, 56; leadership team, 64; local business community, 65; meals, 66; partnerships, 64; staff's emotional well-being, 56–57
caring for students: challenges, 62–63; devices, 61; emotional well-being, 62; in-person learning, 61–63; remote learning, 61–63; team, 61–62
challenges with ESSER, 39–40
Cheatham, Jennifer Perry, 107

children's education, 86, 94
chronic absenteeism, 69, 89–91, 103
chronic attendance, post-pandemic: communication pattern, 92; cultural shift, 91; engaging curriculum, 91; family involvement, 91–92; habit of, 91; health problems, 90; low-cost interventions, 90; percentage of students, 89–90; poverty, 90; pre-pandemic initiatives, 90–91; schools relationships, 92–93; traditional activities, 92; virtual classrooms, 92
Collaborative on Political Leadership in the Superintendency (CPLS), 107
collaborative solutions, 32
combating isolation, 22–23
communicating and partnering, families and community: building trust, 89; chronic attendance, post-pandemic, 89–93; exemplary leadership, Salazar-Zamora, Martha, 101–3; new ways to communicate, 95–96; overview, 85–87; parents, children's first teacher, 93–95; schools and parents relationships, 87–89; synopsis, 103–4; teamwork in planning, 96–100
community-based organizations, 44, 52
community-wide movement, 52
conflicting state and federal guidance, 109–10
confronting post-pandemic challenges: advent of AI, 128–29; evolving role of school boards, 127–28; expansion of school choice and vouchers, 125–27; federal and state overreach, 124–25; final reflections, 130–31; overview, 123; polarization and partisanship, 124; threat of obsolete, 129–30
connecting, power of networking: building relationships, 19–21; combating isolation, 22–23; district teams as networks, 21–22; exemplary leadership, Lee-perera, A. Katrise, 26–29; exemplary leadership, Lubelfeld, Michael, 29–31; exemplary leadership, Polyak, Nick, 29–31; influence of formal networks, 23–26; one-size-fits-all networking, 18–19; overview, 17–18; synopsis, 31–32
Connect Kids Now, 114
COVID-19, 17, 26–29, 124. *See also individual entries*
crisis communications: Day in the Life of (DILO), 5–6, *5–6*; facing criticism, 4; leaders, 3; leadership teams, 5–6; managing information and emotions, 4; schools reopened, 5; school system, 4–6
crisis leadership, 1–2, 7, 121
culture of care, students and staff: caring for staff, 56–58; deploying devices and professional development, 59; exemplary leadership, Gilmore, Kristine, 64–66; exemplary leadership, Rouse, Theresa, 61–63; maintaining connection, 55–56; maintaining staff morale, 60; overview, 51–52; providing meals, 53–54; shifting to remote learning, 52–53; supporting students' emotional well-being, 54–55; synopsis, 66

Davis, Baron R., 7, 40, 108, 114, 115, 125
Davis, Mary Elizabeth, 18
Day in the Life of (DILO), 5–6, *5–6*
decision-making processes, 1, 5, 9, 21, 109, 111–12
deploying devices and professional development, 59
develop long-term plans, 48
district teams as networks, 21–22
dual pandemic, 108

education system, 129–30
effects of COVID-19, school budgets. *See* relief funding and complex legacy

Elementary and Secondary School Emergency Relief Fund (ESSER), 33–34; challenges, 39–40; federal data, 38; learning acceleration, 38; positive impact of, 42–44; primary uses of, 37–38; school budgets before, 36–37; school districts, 38; short-and long-term aims of, 34–36

Enfield, Susan, 54, 57

enterprise superintendent: oil and gas company, 101; programs, 101–3

evolving role of school boards, 127–28

exemplary leadership: ASD's Elementary PM program, 12–13; building relationships, 11; day-to-day decisions, 12; early tracking, 11; education, 9–10; Gilmore, Kristine, 64–66; Gothard, Joe, 117–20; Kerr, Deb, 46–48; Lee-perera, A. Katrise on Sister Supes, 26–29; Lubelfeld, Michael and Polyak, Nick ten years of Supt Chat, 29–31; Miyashiro, David, 79–83; problem-solving, 12–13; Rouse, Theresa, 61–63; Salazar-Zamora, Martha, 101–3; Spicciati, Alan, 10–14; Transition Assistance Program, 11

expansion of inequality, districts: deadlines, 41; financial management perspective, 41–42; initiatives, 41, 42; long-standing needs, 41; resources, 40; spending timelines, 40–41

expansion of school choice and vouchers, 125–27

Fauci, Anthony, 100, 109
federal and state overreach, 124–25
federal relief funding program, 33
Floyd, George, 108, 118, 124
foster collaboration, 48

Generative AI (GenAI), 128
Gilmore, Kristine, 14, 64–66, 115
Goffney, LaTonya, 60, 110, 114

Gothard, Joe, 23, 58, 108, *119*; collaborative approach, 120; innovation, 119; leadership, 119–20; political challenges, 118–19; remote learning, 118; St. Paul Public Schools (SPPS), 117

Great Recession of 2008, 34, 36, 45

Hashtag Supt Chat, 29, 30, *30*
health and safety measures, 37
human connection technology, 66
Hutchings, Gregory, 4, 8, 9, 53, 59, 60, 108

importance of hope and optimism, 10–14
importance of relationships, 70
influence of formal networks, 23–26
innovating to improve education: exemplary leadership, Miyashiro, David, 79–83; overview, 69–71; synopsis, 83–84; teaching and learning during COVID-19, 74–76; teaching and learning post-pandemic, 76–79; teaching and learning pre-COVID-19, 71–74

Johnson-Trammell, Kyla, 52, 110–11, 114, 115

Kerr, Deborah, 94; areas of measurement, 47–48; community church, 47; health and wellness, 46–47; safety and technology, 46; students' needs, 46

Law, David, 77
leaders, 1, 2, 7, 25–26, 69, 111–12
Leadership in a Crisis: Responding to the Coronavirus Outbreak and Future Challenge, 3
lead from your values, 14
learning management systems (LMS), 59, 74
learn responsible transparency, 7; agility and flexibility, 6; honesty

and vulnerability, 8; infection-rate threshold, 7–8; integral part of leadership, 7; leadership comfort zone, 7; life-and-death decisions, 8
Lee-perera, A. Katrise, 26–29
Lubelfeld, Michael, 29–31

maintaining connection, 55–56
maintaining staff morale, 60
maintain transparency, 48
managing local politics, 110–11
managing politics, prioritizing students: advocating for students, 113–14; balancing union and school board relationships, 111–13; conflicting state and federal guidance, 109–10; exemplary leadership, Gothard, Joe, 117–20; managing local politics, 110–11; overview, 107–8; personal toll and enduring consequences, 115–17; rising tensions, 108–9; synopsis, 120–21
massive mobilization, 52
McCain, John S., 96, 97
measuring improvements, 48
mental health, 45–48, 54–55, 60, 78; services, 37
mentorship opportunities, 32
Menzel, Scott A., 42, 44, 88, 90–91
Miller, Matt, 4, 86, 108, 116, 127
mitigating the funding: choices, 45; evidence-based practices, 46; low-income backgrounds, 45; revenue, 45; state funding, 44–45; sustainability, 45; takeaway, 45
monitoring student performance, 47
Muri, Scott, 8, 53

National Assessment of Educational Progress (NAEP), 69
National Center for Education Statistics, 115
National Reopening Listening Tour, 75
National School Lunch Program, 53
new normal, 43, 79

new ways to communicate, 95–96
nimble, 14, 64
no "one-size-fits-all" networking, 18–19

overcommunication, 95

pandemic. *See individual entries*
parents are children's first teacher: caregiver *vs.* educator relationships, 94–95; COVID-19 relief funding, 93; educational realities, 93; family's role in education, 94; parent engagement, 93; partnership, 94; remote learning, 93–94; social and emotional wellness, 94
Pathways in Technology Early College High Schools (P-TECH) programs, 101
personal toll and enduring consequences: emotions, 116; experience, 116–17; ILO Group's Superintendent Research Project (2022), 115; impact of turnover, 115; political battles, 115, 116; Superintendent Lab, 115
polarization and partisanship, 69, 124
political climate, 124, 127
Polyak, Nick, 29–31
positive impact of ESSER funding: benefits, 42–43; broader need, 44; collaboration, 44; collective impact framework, 44; energy and attention, 43; innovative changes, 43; new initiatives, 43; supplemental curriculum, 42
post-pandemic: academic learning, 78; chronic attendance, 89–93; collective planning, 78–79; confronting, 123–31; COVID Keepers, 76–77; districts investement, 77; era, 130; learner-centric, 76, 79; mental health, 78; new normal, 79; Social Emotional Learning (SEL), 78; technology systems, 77–78; tutoring, 78

pre-COVID-19, 51; classrooms, 72; educational reform, 72; forced remote learning, 71; inequalities, 74; mastery-based system, 72–73; school districts, 73; stress, 73; surveys, 73; traditional schedule, 71–72
prioritizing health and safety, 3
priority communication, 48
professional development, 38
providing meals, 53–54
public education, 123, 126–27
public health, 109–10
public schools, 125–26

racism, 108
rapid transition, 53, 79
reflections of, 130; criticism, 131; new and future superintendents, 131; stepped up, 130–31
relief funding and complex legacy: challenges with ESSER, 39–40; ESSER funds, 37–38; exemplary leadership, Kerr, Deb, 46–48; mitigating the funding cliff, 44–46; overview, 33–34; positive impact of ESSER funding, 42–44; school budgets before ESSER, 36–37; short-and long-term aims of ESSER, 34–36; synopsis, 48–49; widened inequality within districts, 40–42
remote learning, 37, 52, 61–63, 75, 80, 111
resource sharing, 32
rising tensions, 108–9

Salazar-Zamora, Martha, 43, 95, 101–3
school board elections matter, 120
school budgets before ESSER, 36–37
school choice movement, 86, 96, 125–26
school district superintendents, 85
school lockdown, 1
schools and parents relationships: centralizing communication strategies, 88; collaboration, 87; feedback, 88; learning rate, 87; level of family involvement, 87–88; meetings, 88–89; technology, 89
school soccer field opening, 1
schools relationship with parents and families, 86
Schuler, David, 9, 19, 35
Scribner, Kent P., 41
service providers, 66
shared experiences, 31
shifting to remote learning, 52–53
short-and long-term aims of ESSER, 34–36
Singh, Candy, 54, 56, 73, 112
Sipe, Heidi, 18, 22
Sister Supes, 26–29
social-emotional learning (SEL), 55, 60, 78
Spence, Aaron, 116, 129–30
Spicciati, Alan, 7, 10–14
State education agencies (SEAs), 34
Stephenson, Carrie, 89
St. Paul Public Schools (SPPS), 117
strength in vulnerability, 14
student engagement, 59, 69, 70, 76
students before politics, 120
superintendents: final reflections, 130–31; health mitigation strategy, 9; lead now and feel later, 9–10; political leaders, 120; Racist Superintendent, 9, *10*; target at times, 9. *See also individual entries*
supporting students emotional well-being, 54–55
Supt Chat, 29–31

teacher professional development, 75
teaching and learning, 3, 129; during COVID-19, 74–76; post-pandemic, 76–79; pre-COVID-19, 71–74
team matters, 66
teamwork in planning: challenges and opportunities, 96; curriculum, 96; educational program, 96, 100; innovation, 100; kindergarten, 100;

learning stair, 97–98; meetings, 96–97; school's physical building, 98–100; terms, 98; virtual meetings, 98
technology and infrastructure, 37, 86
Templeton, Mary, 76, 83
threat of obsolete, 129–30
tracking student attendance and engagement, 48
traditional model of education, 129

virtual learning, 59, 86
voucher programs, 126

White, Rachel, 115
Wilson, Kristi, 96, *99*
words of encouragement, 2

Xiong, Marny, 118, *119*

About the Authors

Susan Enfield is the former superintendent for the Washoe County School District in Reno, Nevada. Prior to this, she spent a decade serving as superintendent for Highline Public Schools in Burien, Washington. During that time, the district developed its Highline Promise to know every student by name, strength, and need so they graduate prepared for the future they choose. A former high school English, journalism, and ELL teacher, Susan served as chief academic officer and then as interim superintendent for Seattle Public Schools before joining Highline in 2012. She previously held leadership positions in Evergreen Public Schools (Vancouver, WA), Portland Public Schools, and the Pennsylvania Department of Education. Susan is a graduate of the University of California, Berkeley, and earned master's degrees from Stanford University and Harvard University. She also holds a doctoral degree in administration, planning, and social policy from Harvard's Urban Superintendents Program. She was named the Superintendent of the Year by the National School Foundation Association in 2018 and was the 2022 Washington State Superintendent of the Year.

Kristi Wilson is a highly regarded educational leader with extensive experience navigating the complexities of public education. Dr. Wilson served over a decade as superintendent in a suburban district, providing invaluable insights into crisis management and leadership. As the former president of AASA, The School Superintendents Association, Dr. Wilson played a pivotal role in advocating for transformative changes in education, as evidenced by her involvement in AASA's "An American Imperative: A New Vision of Public Schools Learning 2025" report commissioned by the U.S. Department of Education. Dr. Wilson has authored numerous articles on topics ranging from crisis leadership to community engagement, including publications such as Leadership for Smooth Sailing: Navigating Educational Challenges in Times of Crisis and Redefining the Paradigm in Elementary and Secondary Education. Her expertise and dedication to fostering innovation and resilience in education make Dr. Wilson a leading voice in shaping the future of public education. She was named Superintendent of the Year for the National VH1 Save the Music Program in 2015 and was the 2021 Arizona Superintendent of the Year.